Utilizing New Information Technology in Teaching of International Business: A Guide for Instructors

Utilizing New Information Technology in Teaching of International Business: A Guide for Instructors

Fahri Karakaya, PhD
Erdener Kaynak, PhD
Editors

International Business Press
An Imprint of
The Haworth Press, Inc.
New York • London • Norwood (Australia)

656.049
U89

Utilizing New Information Technology in Teaching of International Business: A Guide for Instructors has also been published as *Journal of Teaching in International Business,* Volume 4, Numbers 3/4 1993.

The Haworth Press, Inc., 10 Alice Street, Binghamton, NY 13904-1580 USA

Library of Congress Cataloging-in-Publication Data

Utilizing new information technology in teaching of international business : a guide for instructors / Fahri Karakaya, Erdener Kaynak, editors.
    p. cm.
    Includes bibliographical references.
    ISBN 1-56024-416-X (alk. paper)
    1. International business enterprises–Study and teaching–Data processing. 2. Business education–Data processing. I. Karakaya, Fahri. II. Kaynak, Erdener.
HD62.4.U89 1993
658'.049'0715–dc20
                                                                                          93-27148
                                                                                          CIP

INDEXING & ABSTRACTING

Contributions to this publication are selectively indexed or abstracted in print, electronic, online, or CD-ROM version(s) of the reference tools and information services listed below. This list is current as of the copyright date of this publication. See the end of this section for additional notes.

- *Contents Pages in Education*, Carfax Information Systems, PO Box 25, Abingdon, Oxfordshire, OX14 3UE, United Kingdom

- *Contents Pages in Management*, University of Manchester Business School, Booth Street West, Manchester, M15 6PB, England

- *Educational Technology Abstracts*, Carfax Publishing Company, PO Box 25, Abingdon, Oxfordshire OX14 3UE, United Kingdom

- *Index to Periodical Articles Related to Law*, University of Texas, 727 East 26th Street, Austin, TX 78705

- *International Bulletin of Bibliography on Education*, Proyecto B.I.B.E./Apartado 52, San Lorenzo del Escorial, Madrid, Spain

- *Linguistics and Language Behavior Abstracts (LLBA)*, Sociological Abstracts, Inc., PO Box 22206, San Diego, CA 92192-0206

- *Management & Marketing Abstracts*, Pira International, Randalls Road, Leatherhead, Surrey KT22 7RU, England

- *Social Planning/Policy & Development Abstracts (SOPODA)*, Sociological Abstracts, Inc., PO Box 22206, San Diego, CA 92192-0206

- *Sociological Abstracts (SA)*, Sociological Abstracts, Inc., PO Box 22206, San Diego, CA 92192-0206

- *Technical Education & Training Abstracts*, Carfax Publishing Company, PO Box 25, Abingdon, Oxfordshire OX14 3UE, United Kingdom

(continued)

SPECIAL BIBLIOGRAPHIC NOTES

related to indexing and abstracting

- [ ] indexing/abstracting services in this list will also cover material in the "separate" that is co-published simultaneously with Haworth's special thematic journal issue or DocuSerial. Indexing/abstracting usually covers material at the article/chapter level.

- [ ] monographic co-editions are intended for either non-subscribers or libraries which intend to purchase a second copy for their circulating collections.

- [ ] monographic co-editions are reported to all jobbers/wholesalers/approval plans. The source journal is listed as the "series" to assist the prevention of duplicate purchasing in the same manner utilized for books-in-series.

- [ ] to facilitate user/access services all indexing/abstracting services are encouraged to utilize the co-indexing entry note indicated at the bottom of the first page of each article/chapter/contribution.

- [ ] this is intended to assist a library user of any reference tool (whether print, electronic, online, or CD-ROM) to locate the monographic version if the library has purchased this version but not a subscription to the source journal.

- [ ] individual articles/chapters in any Haworth publication are also available through the Haworth Document Delivery Services (HDDS).

Utilizing New Information Technology in Teaching of International Business: A Guide for Instructors

CONTENTS

ABOUT THE EDITORS

Fahri Karakaya, PhD, MBA, is Associate Professor of Marketing and Director of the MBA program at the University of Massachusetts Dartmouth. He has conducted numerous consulting projects in the areas of market entry and marketing research and operates the Market Research and Data Analysis Group, a marketing research firm in Westport, Massachusetts. The author of the book *Barriers to Entry* and *Market Entry Decisions: A Guide to Marketing Executives*, Dr. Karakaya has published in the *Journal of Marketing* and other refereed journals and has made numerous presentations in national conferences. His many research interests include strategic marketing, marketing research techniques, consumer behavior, and computers and marketing education. He was chair of the 1991 American Marketing Association Micro-computers in Marketing Education National Conference. Dr. Karakaya is a member of the American Marketing Association, the Academy of Marketing Science, the Academy of Management, and the International Management Development Association.

Erdener Kaynak, PhD, is Professor of Marketing at the School of Business Administration of The Pennsylvania State University at Harrisburg. He has held key teaching and administrative positions in Europe, Asia, and North America.

Professor Kaynak has extensive consultancy and advisory experience in the international marketing area in a number of countries in Europe, North and Latin America, the Middle East, and the Far East. He has conducted post-doctoral research studies and held executive training programs around the world, and founded and headed a consulting firm in Halifax, Nova Scotia. While Director of International Programs and on the Board of Governors of the Academy of Marketing Science, he organized two World Marketing Congresses.

The recipient of numerous research awards, scholarships and distinctions, Dr. Kaynak is author or co-author of some 12 books and over 100 scholarly publications in the field of international marketing and cross-cultural/national consumer behavior. Dr. Kaynak serves on the editorial review boards of some leading marketing/management journals and is currently Senior Editor, International Business, for The Haworth Press, Inc. He is also the editor of several other Haworth periodicals, including the *Journal of Global Marketing*, the *Journal of International Consumer Marketing*, the *Journal of Food & Agribusiness Marketing*, and the *Journal of Teaching in International Business*.

Acknowledgements

I wish to acknowledge Dr. Erdener Kaynak for his direction and support in developing the collection. The assistance provided at the University of Massachusetts Dartmouth by Dean Harold L. Gilmore and Denise Rebeiro is greatly appreciated. Special thanks go to Kate Jones-Randall, Laura Joshi, Erik Sylvia, and Steve Swan for their continued support in this and other projects. Finally, this publication would not have been possible without the following reviewers' diligent contributions.

Barry Berman, Hofstra University
Satya P. Chattopadhyay, University of Scranton
Jean C. Darian, Rider College
Andrew M. Forman, Hofstra University
Ron Green, East Tennessee State University
Greg Gundlach, University of Notre Dame
Helen LaFrancois, University of Massachusetts Dartmouth
Michael Laric, University of Baltimore
Kamlesh T. Mehta, St. Mary's University
Linda J. Morris, University of Idaho
Richard E. Plank, University of Massachusetts-Lowell
Carolyn E. Predmore, Manhattan College
Linda Ann Riley, New Mexico State University
Ronald S. Rubin, University Central Florida
Alok Srivastava, Georgia State University
Margery Steinberg, University of Hartford
Ercan Tirtiroglu, University of Massachusetts Dartmouth
Lewis R. Tucker, University of Hartford
John Weber, University of Notre Dame
Eddie Yasin, East Tennessee State University

Fahri Karakaya
University of Massachusetts Dartmouth

Introduction

Erdener Kaynak

In today's competitive global market arena, firms of all sizes are trying to internationalize their activities. To be able to gain competitive edge over their competitors, U.S. firms as well as firms from other countries constantly need and search for data and information about markets they contemplate entry into as well as the ones they are currently operating. In this process, firms from different industries try to gain distinct advantages to remain competitive. One of these differentiation tools is information techniques and tools.

In view of its increased importance, this publication is devoted to International Business Education in the Information Age. Under the very able editorship of Professor Fahri Karakaya of the University of Massachusetts–Dartmouth, an excellent volume was created. Besides managerially-oriented articles, there are also two software reviews. All of the contributors represent state-of-the-art reviews and contributions to the growing field of international business. I offer my heartfelt congratulations to Professor Fahri Karakaya for bringing this project to a very successful fruition.

The first article offered by Professor Karakaya sets the foundation for the volume. During the last decade or so, teaching, research as well as practise of international business have shown remarkable changes. This has stemmed from the increased emphasis placed on

[Haworth co-indexing entry note]: "Introduction." Kaynak, Erdener. Co-published simultaneously in the *Journal of Teaching in International Business* (The Haworth Press, Inc.) Vol. 4, No. 3/4, 1993, pp. 1-7; and: *Utilizing New Information Technology in Teaching of International Business: A Guide for Instructors* (ed: Fahri Karakaya and Erdener Kaynak) The Haworth Press, Inc., 1993, pp. 1-7. Multiple copies of this article/chapter may be purchased from The Haworth Document Delivery Center. Call 1-800-3-HAWORTH (1-800-342-9678) between 9:00 - 5:00 (EST) and ask for DOCUMENT DELIVERY CENTER.

global business by the U.S. government agencies and firms alike and recent innovations in computer and information systems technology.

Academicians, practitioners, as well as public policy makers in developed and developing countries have been working together in developing new teaching tools and techniques to improve and advance the way international business subjects are taught. For instance, recent developments in the areas of computer data bases such as DSS (Decision Support Systems), simulation games, and expert systems have all added a different dimension to the business administration curriculum. In the U.S.A., the AACSB (American Assembly of Collegiate Schools of Business) guidelines have also influenced the new and innovative teaching methods employed by colleges and universities in both undergraduate and graduate business education by incorporating international business practises into the business curiculum.

The paper by Bhargava et al. is directed towards teachers, students, business executives and managers who are confronted with international business situations every day. During one of the first phases of internationalization, market assessment plays an important role. Managers have to select target markets, analyze them and come up with the most feasible markets. Searching for information for the above analysis may be a difficult task and can take a lot of time.

Country Consultant is an intelligent database, that is being developed to assist managers in these situations. This decision support tool brings international business and artificial intelligence (AI) expertise together. The paper has been written from the perspective of Country Consultant being used as an educational tool. After a brief literature review in the first section, the second section provides a brief introduction to this database. From this section, readers can get a good understanding about the organization of this database, type of information available, and the different AI features of Country Consultant. Country Consultant has been used in some international business classes as an educational tool. Experience of using this database in classrooms is discussed in the next section. This section discusses the strategy used for teaching students market research, how this strategy has been refined in the last one year of its use, how students have added to their learning experience and the criteria used to evaluate students. In the end conclusions are made about the use of Country Consultant as an intelligent database and experiences of using it in the classroom for education purposes.

The article by George V. Priovolos evaluates one of the first entries on the market for international business/marketing educational software, "Export To Win!" (ETW). The program, originally developed to assist medium-sized businesses in learning the export process, places the user in the position of the marketing manager of a manufacturing firm with two industrial products. S/he has to develop an export plan for the company to become a successful global competitor and reach its stated goal of $6 million in export revenues within the next five years.

With regard to ETW's learning objectives, the program's strengths lie primarily in (a) providing students with a realistic account of the way small- and medium-sized businesses may engage in international marketing; (b) acquainting them with some basic sources of international marketing information; (c) introducing users to the language and specialized terms of international trade, and (d) emphasizing the importance of proper marketing planning and on-going market research in achieving success in international marketing. Prospective adopters of ETW will also appreciate the program's simplicity and overall user-friendliness which make it easy to use even by students with limited computer experience.

On the other hand, the most significant weaknesses of ETW are (a) its atomistic/one-player orientation and (b) the limited amount of challenging decision-making required by the software. In the view of the author, ETW is mis-positioned as an export simulation game to the degree that the program offers student-users little opportunity to explore different hypotheses in international marketing and examine the desirability of diverse policy alternatives by doing.

The article concludes by reviewing several features that future educational software in the area of international business/marketing should incorporate to contribute in a meaningful way to the teaching of an increasingly expanding but also indispensable subject.

The performance of U.S. companies in the international trade arena has been poor in comparison to our major trading partners. Surprisingly, only 15% of all U.S. manufacturers actually export. This relatively poor performance occurs despite the federal government's extensive efforts to promote international trade. Part of the problem has been the inability to effectively package and distribute to potential users the tremendous volume of information on the exporting process maintained by public and private sources. Aided by the increased availability and acceptance of personal computers, however, several software developers and the federal government have recently introduced programs which are highly effective in organizing and retrieving the massive amounts of information available on the exporting process. The paper by Kearns and Schmitt analyzes five such ground-breaking software programs with an eye to their utility as teaching tools to meet the diverse needs of individual users.

In the selection of a program, two evaluative criteria were utilized. (a) The first one was a broad based coverage of the export process which enables business administration students and business practitioners to use it as a comprehensive educational or training tool. (b) The program can be run by a personal computer. Along this particular criteria, only five programs could be used. These programs, which were highly specific in nature and related to a certain aspect of the export process, were excluded since they would not be appropriate as a comprehensive educational tool. The authors also develop several hypothetical case studies to show similarities and/or differences among five software programs and to point out their potential as a guide to be used by educators, advisors, and businessmen.

The paper by Miller and Miller examines the potential for electronic data retrieval techniques in international business courses. It assesses the current status of these techniques and the costs associated with using them for classroom purposes. It also describes the two alternative forms of electronic data retrieval, online data retrieval and CD ROM systems.

Following this general discussion, the paper focuses on each of the two available technologies, identifying specific database sources for each that might be used in various international business classes.

The paper concludes that the wide range of information resources available in these electronic formats and the reasonable and decreasing costs of accessing those resources render electronic information retrieval a most valuable microcomputer application in the international business classroom.

In recent years several international financial databases have become available and can be accessed by multinational enterprises as well as researchers and educators. The objective of the article by Abdel M. Agami is to illustrate how these databases can be used by students in international accounting courses in surveying the accounting and financial reporting practices of corporations in foreign countries.

Each student chooses a foreign country as well as a corporation from that foreign country along with a similar U.S. corporation. At the second stage, the student researches and critically examines the cultural, economic business environments and the accounting standards of the foreign country and the accounting standards as well as accounting practices of the foreign and U.S. Corporations. The student is asked to point out whether the differences in accounting standards and practices between a foreign country and the U.S.A. have hindered the students's views as to how to overcome the national barriers. It is hoped that this project exposes students to the cultural, economic, and business practices in other countries and gives them a chance to appreciate the diversity in the global economy that they are soon to become part of.

Information provided in the evaluation of Harper and Bush should benefit teachers of International Business who are considering requiring students' use of computerized data sources or teachers who already require such interaction but have not used one or more of the sources evaluated herein. Based on the results, the authors recommend time be devoted to a review of the on-line library catalogue system, if available. Secondly, given the constraints of an assigned class project requiring specific market and trade data on various countries, teachers should consider the relatively new National Trade Data Bank (NTDB). Information provided by the NTDB was far superior to information from any other source. Finally, there is the interesting simulation now available, "Export To Win!", which provides information essential in exporting goods within the context of a traditional simulation. Student evaluations of the simulation were positive.

In the last two articles, two softwares were critically analyzed and reviewed for the benefit of our readers. The first one is reviewed by Nicholls and Comer. *The Management of Strategy in a Global Market Place* is a microcomputer simulation that has great promise for teaching international business. The simulation is unusually complex and realistic. Using microcomputers as a generic product, participants research the potential markets in five regions of the world, identify user segments, and design individual brands. Each team (4-5 players) operates companies for a 2-3 year period, at the instructor's discretion. Their task is to produce the product in their own factories and to distribute it to the ultimate consumer through a network of warehouses and retail outlets. They may expand operations, invest in R&D, and produce products in different quality levels. They make decisions involving production, marketing, and finance. All this occurs in a competitive environment involving global economic and cultural factors.

The simulation involves role play as well as computer aspects. The associated role play can be as elaborate as an instructor chooses. Teams can negotiate with each other, can merge or acquire each other, can monitor each other's activities. They are also able to license technology from competitors.

Reactions to an earlier version of the simulation indicate that the students perceived multiple benefits ranging from having a realistic experience to the development of interpersonal skills. When compared to another recent simulation, "Export To Win!", *The Global Market Place* was found to be quite different and aimed at a different market. The simulation is suitable for a capstone course in international business or for an executive training program.

The increase in international business enrollments has changed the pedagogical focus of internal business courses and helped internationalize the curriculum in many business schools. But there is a need to incorporate more computerized databases on the international operations of firms in order to stimulate student interest and coordinate the internationalization of functions.

The software paper by John William Clarry reviews the coverage and software capabilities of two databases available for international business education from Compact Disclosure and World-scope/Disclosure. While the former offers extensive data from the annual reports of over 10,000 public firms, most of these are U.S. owned and do not provide many explicit international business variables. The latter database from Worldscope/Disclosure offers records from over 6000 firms from mostly non-U.S. nations, which have rarely been available online before. Despite some limits from software and search fields, the extensive foreign business statistics on sales, income, assets, and growth provide abundant current data for international business research. The final section proposes database applications for several student research projects for different functional disciplines with international scope. The easy use of these databases for such projects should stimulate more student interest beyond case studies, and further the internationalization of the skills and curriculum of business schools.

Teaching International Business in the Information Age: State of the Art

Fahri Karakaya

SUMMARY. Teaching international business has changed during the last decade because of the emphasis placed on global business by the U.S. government and innovations in computer technology. Academicians and practitioners have been working together in developing new teaching tools to improve the way we teach international business. Recent developments in the areas of computer databases, simulation games and expert systems have added a different dimension to the business curriculum. The AACSB guidelines in incorporating international business practices into the business curriculum have also influenced the new teaching methods employed by colleges and universities in both undergraduate and graduate business education in the U.S.A.

INTRODUCTION

Almost all colleges and universities in the U.S. have been trying to integrate computers into their business curriculum. Lower prices

Fahri Karakaya is Associate Professor of Marketing and Director of the MBA Program at the University of Massachusetts–Dartmouth, North Dartmouth, MA 02747.

[Haworth co-indexing entry note]: "Teaching International Business in the Information Age: State of the Art." Karakaya, Fahri. Co-published simultaneously in the *Journal of Teaching in International Business* (The Haworth Press, Inc.) Vol. 4, No. 3/4, 1993, pp. 9-16; and: *Utilizing New Information Technology in Teaching of International Business: A Guide for Instructors* (ed: Fahri Karakaya and Erdener Kaynak) The Haworth Press, Inc., 1993, pp. 9-16. Multiple copies of this article/ chapter may be purchased from The Haworth Document Delivery Center. Call 1-800-3-HAWORTH (1-800-342-9678) between 9:00 - 5:00 (EST) and ask for DOCUMENT DELIVERY CENTER.

of hardware and software, and availability of qualified user support personnel at college or university computer centers have facilitated and accelerated this integration in the last decade. According to the Eighth Annual UCLA Survey of Business School Computer Usage (Frand and Britt 1991), 164 schools reported having a total of 35,228 microcomputers ranging from 16 to 830 per school with an average of 215 microcomputers. Figure 1 shows the average system per school and average percentage growth from 1985 to 1991. The average system per school has almost tripled from 1986 to 1991. However, as one would expect the average growth rate has slowed down from 64% in 1986 to 7% in 1991.

In addition to microcomputer availability, 95 percent of the business schools surveyed said that their users had access to mini/

Figure 1
Microcomputer Availability and Annual Growth Rate at Business Schools*

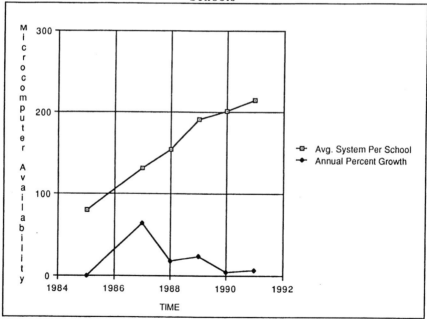

*Data Obtained from the Eighth Annual UCLA Survey of Business School Computer Usage

mainframe computer systems. Consistent with the increased number of microcomputers available for both students and faculty, the percentage of business schools requiring computer usage in core courses has increased from 60% in 1985 to 73% in 1991 (percentages include the average of all core courses). The increase in the percentage of schools requiring computer usage in graduate core courses is somewhat lower than the percentage increase in undergraduate core courses. The percentage of schools requiring computer usage in their graduate core courses has gone up from 57% in 1985 to 66% (9% increase versus 13% increase in the undergraduate core courses). Among the undergraduate core courses, the largest increase in the percentage of schools requiring computer usage has been in management science courses (29% increase from 1985 to 1991) while the smallest increase has been in production/operations management courses (only one percentage increase from 1985 to 1991).

From the data presented in the Annual UCLA Survey of Business School Computer Usage, it is clear that more and more business schools are integrating computers into both their undergraduate and graduate curriculums. In addition to the advances in technology, lower cost, and user support assistance provided at colleges and universities, ability to use computers is considered fundamental for the well-educated individual. According to Bush and Burns (1984), this is the major reason for adopting and integrating microcomputers into the business curriculum.

A variety of business courses have easily adopted computer usage. The courses listed as requiring computers in the Eighth Annual UCLA Survey of Business School Computer Usage (Frand and Britt 1991) include the following: Accounting, Business Policy, Economics, Finance, Information Systems, Management Science, Marketing, Organization Behavior, Production and Operations Management, and Statistics. Interestingly, the list does not include any international business courses. It is possible that international business courses are not yet core courses in many institutions, and not included in the survey. The UCLA Survey does not mention teaching international business or any related issue except an international database package use. Four years ago, in the U.S., 118 undergraduate and 94 graduate business schools required students to take at least one international business course (Beamish 1988). These numbers are likely to be much higher today. In a more recent survey of 50 major U.S. universities, Kuhne (1990) found 28 offering doctoral programs with a major, minor, or concentration in international business.

INTERNATIONALIZATION OF THE BUSINESS CURRICULUM

In internationalization of business curriculum, Larson (1991), claims that most business programs in the U.S. have added an international marketing course as a quick fix. International marketing courses, however, are not enough to internationalize the business curriculum. A study of 127 U.S. firms with international operations showed that most firms preferred international managers with overseas experience, but international business finance, accounting and law, academic or special executive development training serves as a close substitute for overseas experience (Reynolds and Rice 1988). However, Finney and Von Glinow claim that neither academic nor organizational approaches are preparing U.S. managers adequately for successful careers as international managers. These researchers propose joint programs undertaken by organizations and business schools.

A survey of 122 major Canadian firms indicated that international business skills were more relevant after some work experience had been obtained (Beamish and Calof 1989). Furthermore, the respondents in this study ranked business degrees and engineering highest for students preparing for international careers. According to the executives participating in the study, the most important courses were international marketing and sales, international finance and capital markets, and international trade and export management. Boyd, Clark, and Lewis (1990) present a different view and claim that the basic business communication course can be used effectively as one way to provide students with an adequate focus of the international dimension.

Some U.S. colleges and universities have changed their traditional way of teaching international business. Some universities utilize student exchange programs and overseas field trips more often than they have earlier. Short overseas programs such as the two-week summer course in Reims, France, offered by Northeastern University expose graduate students to experiential learning in overseas environment (Sarathy 1990). Texas Christian University's study abroad program in Cologne, Germany is another successful example of such programs (Boatler 1990). Other universities and colleges also have similar programs in both graduate and undergraduate international business education. Northern State University in South Dakota began a new international business major within the school of business in 1989. According to Hendon (1989), the objectives of the program are to (1) prepare students to understand America's trading partners, and (2) teach the technical knowledge needed in international business environment. This program is only open to highly motivated students with above-average scholastic achievement.

UTILIZING COMPUTERS IN TEACHING OF INTERNATIONAL BUSINESS COURSES

Other major changes in teaching international business include the use of micro and mainframe computers. A variety of international business courses utilize databases and other computerized instructional tools in developing a better understanding of the international business environment. The availability of diverse database packages, simulation games, and expert systems have made integration of computers into teaching international business courses possible.

Computer Databases

There are at least six international database packages currently available in the market. Some of these databases are easily accessible and at low cost, making their integration into the international business courses possible.

National Trade Data Bank. This is probably the most popular database that is utilized in international business courses. It is available from the U.S. Department of Commerce and updated monthly. Universities and colleges with Federal Government Collections already have this database. It contains approximately 100,000 documents from CIA, Federal Reserve System, Ex-Im Bank, and Overseas Private Investment Corporation.

Disclosure/Worldscope. This database has data on 6,000 companies from 24 countries. It is similar to Lotus database available in many university libraries. SIC codes and industry names can be used for searching and identifying new markets. It contains data on sales, income and growth rates, foreign assets, return on assets, and asset turnover.

Word Trade Exporter. Provides link to over 850 external data bases. It is designed to aid small and medium sized U.S. businesses. It has 160 trade topics, a trade directory, a trade bibliography, and a notepad used for editing and note taking purposes.

World Trader. Profiles 125 countries and supplies regional maps. In addition, it lists 2,500 international trade shows and analyzes trade data by country.

PC Globe/MacGlobe. This database contains geographical, demographical, political, climate, currency conversion, and economic information on 190 countries. It also has an atlas with geographic databases.

Electronic data Retrieval (CD-ROM and On-Line Data Retrieval). An example of this type of service is well-known as the "Dialog Business Connection." Using this service can be costly to novice consumers since they have to pay for time logged onto the system. Some examples of the data bases that exist in the Dialog Business Connection include Dun and Bradstreet International, Business International, Infomat International Business, and PTS International Forecasts.

Computer Simulation

Currently there is only a single simulation package, "Export to Win!" for use in international business courses. This simulation software is marketed by Southwest Publishing Company. It is well-known and widely used in international business courses. It is designed to help students understand the exporting practice.

Expert Systems

The "Country Consultant" is the only expert systems software available for use in international business courses. Presently, this software is in the developmental stage and it has been only used as a teaching tool. It includes 39 markets, 98 industries, and 11 entry modes into international markets. It is mainly an application of artificial intelligence to international marketing.

DISCUSSION AND CONCLUSIONS

As the number of available international databases, simulation games and expert systems increases, the number of users will also increase. In utilizing the recent developments in international business courses, it is necessary for faculty teaching international business courses to commit themselves to spend time learning these developments. In addition, adequate user support is needed to assist faculty and students.

The databases mentioned in this report and others can be used to assign student term projects intended to gather data on foreign countries, foreign competition, and methods of exporting overseas. It is important, however, to educate the users of the databases about database accuracy! As pointed out by Mahmoud and Rice (1988) there are some practices followed by database suppliers that could produce unreliable information. Thus, it might sometimes be necessary to verify the gathered information in other databases.

Instructors of international business courses can utilize computer simulation games and expert systems in an attempt to meet the needs of businesses and better train students for the real world. Again, user support is needed to assist faculty and students integrating the simulation games or expert systems packages especially when faculty and students first begin to use them. Using the computer simulation games, expert systems or even the data bases requires a considerable amount of time investment on the behalf of the faculty. However, once the computer assisted teaching tools are learned, the rewards are worth the investment.

REFERENCES

Beamish, Paul W. (1988). A Gap in the Business Curriculum, *Canadian Business Review,* 15 (Winter), 28-30.

_____ and Jonathan L. Calof (1989). International Business Education: A Corporate View, *Journal of International Business Studies,* 20 (3), 553-64.

Boatler, Robert (1990). Study Abroad: Impact on Student Worldmindedness, *Journal of Teaching in International Business,* 2 (2), 17-23.

Boyd, Daniel R., W. Clark Ford, and Stephen D. Lewis (1990). Incorporating International Business Concepts into the Basic Business Communication Course, *Bulletin of the Association for Business Communication,* 53 (4), 59-61.

Finney, Michael and Mary Ann Von Glinow (1988). Integrating Academic and Organizational Approaches to Developing the International Manager, *Journal of Management Development,* 7 (2), 16-27.

Frand, Jason L. and Julia A. Britt (1991). *Eighth Annual UCLA Survey of Business School Computer Usage,* Los Angles, CA: The John E. Anderson Graduate School of Management at UCLA.

Hendon, Donald W. (1989). *International Business Studies,* Washington, DC: American Association of State Colleges and Universities; Aberdeen, SD, Northern State University.

Kuhne, Robert J. (1990). Comparative Analysis of U.S. Doctoral Programs in International Business, *Journal of Teaching in International Business,* 1 (3-4), 85-99.

Larson, Clifford E. (1991). Globalization of Business Curriculum and International Marketing: Symbiotic or Antithetic, *Journal of Teaching in International Business,* 3 (2), 19-27.

Mahmoud, Essam and Gillian Rice (1988). Database Accuracy: Results from a Survey of Database Vendors, *Information and Management,* 15, 243-50.

Reynolds, John I. and George H. Rice (1988). American Education for International Business, *Management International Review,* 28 (3), 48-57.

Sarathy, Ravi (1990). Internationalizing MBA Education: The Role of Short Overseas Programs, *Journal of Teaching in International Business,* 1 (3-4), 101-18.

Using an Intelligent Database in the Classroom: The Case of the Country Consultant

Vivek Bhargava
Cuneyt Evirgen
Michel Mitri
S. Tamer Cavusgil

SUMMARY. This article presents the use, in a classroom setting, of a computer program containing a database of international market information. This program, the Country Consultant, utilizes artificial intelligence techniques for evaluating potential international markets for various industries.

The article discusses issues of market selection, concentrating on the information needs for this task. Then the Country Consultant is described, including its conceptual structure and inferencing capabilities. Finally, we discuss the ways in which Country Consultant has been used in university-level international marketing classes, and the benefits that can be gained from its use.

Vivek Bhargava, Cuneyt Evirgen, Michel Mitri, and S. Tamer Cavusgil are all associated with the International Business Center, Michigan State University.

Address all correspondence to Professor S. Tamer Cavusgil, Executive Director, International Business Centers, Michigan State University, 6 Kellogg Center, East Lansing, MI 48824-1022.

[Haworth co-indexing entry note]: "Using an Intelligent Database in the Classroom: The Case of the Country Consultant." Bhargava, Vivek et al.. Co-published simultaneously in the *Journal of Teaching in International Business* (The Haworth Press, Inc.) Vol. 4, No. 3/4, 1993, pp. 17-37; and: *Utilizing New Information Technology in Teaching of International Business: A Guide for Instructors* (ed: Fahri Karakaya and Erdener Kaynak) The Haworth Press, Inc., 1993, pp. 17-37. Multiple copies of this article/chapter may be purchased from The Haworth Document Delivery Center. Call 1-800-3-HAWORTH (1-800-342-9678) between 9:00 - 5:00 (EST) and ask for DOCUMENT DELIVERY CENTER.

17

INTRODUCTION

This article describes the use, in a classroom setting, of a computer program called the Country Consultant. The Country Consultant is an intelligent database designed to aid international marketing professionals in dealing with market evaluation and selection issues. It was developed at the International Business Centers (IBC) of Michigan State University (MSU).[1]

The term "intelligent database" refers to a class of database structures and querying methods that employ techniques from artificial intelligence (AI). These AI techniques are employed to deal with uncertainty and incompleteness in the content of the database. Thus, intelligent databases commonly *infer* responses to queries for which there is no explicit data (Frisch and Allen, 1989). The Country Consultant is, by this definition, an intelligent database. Its inference method is briefly described later in this article.

As information becomes more complex and decision-making time frames grow shorter, the need to merge AI with database technologies will continue to grow (Brodie, 1989). The Country Consultant brings these technologies together in an attempt to aid the decision-making process in international marketing. In this way, it serves as a valuable tool supporting the counselling and advisory tasks at IBC.

IBC is an organization devoted to encouraging and aiding American businesses to market their products and services internationally. This is done through education, research, community outreach, and one-on-one counselling. The Country Consultant has been used to aid in the counselling efforts at IBC. In addition, it serves as a pedagogical tool for teaching international marketing to MSU students. In this article, we concentrate on the use of Country Consultant in a classroom setting.

INFORMATION REQUIREMENTS IN COUNTRY SELECTION

Information[2] is an input that reduces uncertainty, which is a prevailing factor when entering a foreign environment. In fact,

Davidson (1983) has found that uncertainty is a key factor in market selection decisions. The findings of his study suggest that firms significantly prefer markets similar to the home market, but as they gain experience in a variety of markets this preference declines since uncertainty is decreased through accumulated information and knowledge. The need for information in determining and assessing foreign market opportunities is well supported in the literature (Bodur, 1986; Cavusgil, 1985; Daser, 1984; Keng and Jivan, 1989; Johanson and Vahlne, 1977; Walters, 1983). Information problems may be twofold: either lack of it or being overloaded with it. Cavusgil (1987) notes that international marketers have difficulty in sorting out the relevant, reliable, and timely pieces of information.

Information Frameworks in the Literature

In the literature, various models are proposed categorizing the information needs of firms in assessing and selecting foreign markets for entry. However, empirical studies in this area have been relatively rare. While the terminology or wording is different in the classifications, proposed frameworks of information requirements conceptually overlap.

Some authors have offered general frameworks for information requirements in international marketing and country selection for entry (Davidson, 1983; Douglas and Craig, 1988; Hutcheson, 1984; Jobber, 1982; Keegan, 1984; Staudt et al., 1976). These frameworks do not focus on a particular entry mode. Other frameworks have been proposed that particularly relate to information requirements for country assessment in selecting *export* markets (Bodur and Cavusgil, 1984; Cavusgil, 1984a, 1984b, 1985; Daser, 1984; Kahler, 1983; Trip, 1985; Walters, 1983; Wood and Goolsby, 1987). Furthermore, Ehrman and Hamburg (1986) have studied information requirements for country selection in *foreign direct investment*. The need for initial screening and the related information are also discussed in some of the studies mentioned above (Cavusgil, 1984b, 1985; Daser, 1984; Douglas and Craig, 1988; Ehrman and Hamburg, 1986; Kahler, 1983). All of these frameworks include various constructs or information categories which are briefly described below (see Evirgen, 1990, for a detailed description of each of these frameworks).

In the literature, the importance of obtaining information on the demographic, political, economic, cultural and legal environments has been emphasized by various authors (Bodur and Cavusgil, 1984; Cavusgil, 1984b; Cavusgil, 1985; Daser, 1984; Douglas and Craig, 1988; Ehrman and Hamburg, 1986; Hutcheson, 1984; Jobber, 1982; Kahler, 1983; Keegan, 1984; Staudt et al., 1976; Walters, 1983; Wood and Goolsby, 1987). Trip (1985), on the other hand, mentions environmental information in a broad sense and does not describe which types of information should be included.

Moreover, information on market entry conditions is also mentioned as a required information category (Cavusgil, 1984b; Cavusgil, 1985; Daser, 1984; Kahler, 1983; Keegan, 1984; Wood and Goolsby, 1987). Finally, a review of the information frameworks offered in the literature suggests that although information on the market structure is mentioned in all of the previous studies, it is either defined differently or conceptualized in very different levels of aggregation. For example, Wood and Goolsby (1987) describe it in terms of competitive information, whereas, information on competition and information on market structure are identified as separate information categories by Daser (1984), Kahler (1983), and Keegan (1984).

Furthermore, some authors point out the need to obtain information on particular market structure characteristics such as market size and composition, financial aspects, distribution, etc. (Davidson, 1983; Douglas and Craig, 1988; Ehrman and Hamburg, 1986; Jobber, 1982; Tripp, 1985).

Moreover, Cavusgil (1985) has found that the information requirements of firms tend to follow a three step sequential process. The process starts with *preliminary screening* using broad environmental factors, such as political, economic, cultural, and demographic environments. The second step includes obtaining information for *industry market potential analysis.* Finally, specific information regarding *company sales potential analysis* is obtained (Cavusgil, 1985).

To summarize, information on the demographic, political, economic, cultural, and legal environments, as well as information on market entry conditions and information on the market structure (in aggregate or desegregate form) are pointed out in the literature as the principal information requirements in the evaluation of foreign market attractiveness, and consequently, in foreign country selection for entry. As it will be described later, these information categories have been used as the starting point in designing the feature hierarchy in the Country Consultant. That is, the information categories identified in the literature have been mapped onto a feature hierarchy in the Country Consultant.

On the other hand, there are some conclusions that can be drawn from the literature: (1) various models are proposed categorizing the information needs of firms in assessing and selecting foreign markets for entry; (2) empirical studies in this area have been relatively rare; (3) the terminology or wording is not the same in the proposed classifications; (4) the proposed frameworks tend to be incomprehensive in defining information requirements in evaluating foreign market attractiveness; and (5) the proposed frameworks of information requirements *conceptually overlap*.

THE COUNTRY CONSULTANT

Realizing the deficiency of relevant, reliable, and meaningful information in international business about foreign markets, a decision support tool was developed by a team of researchers at Michigan State University's International Business Centers (IBC) to serve as an information base to the international manager. This decision support tool, called the Country Consultant,[3] brings international business and artificial intelligence (AI) expertise together. The product is an intelligent database designed to aid the international business executive in decision-making, particularly with respect to target market evaluation and selection. It incorporates both business executive insights and market research findings. The software tool is usable with personal computers.

The Country Consultant is an innovative product of ongoing research in AI applications in international marketing. The tool provides market information for key trading partners of the United States. Our tool is unlike readily available databases in that it does not contain statistical or demographic data in a raw form, nor is it merely a collection of textual reports and documents. Rather, it incorporates *judg-*

ments and *guidelines* pertaining to various aspects of the countries in question, and is catalogued according to specific markets, industries, entry modes, and features relevant to market-selection.

In other words, the Country Consultant contains processed information in the form of qualitative, judgmental knowledge. The ultimate purpose of this knowledge is to aid the end-user (presumably someone without an in-depth understanding of the target markets) to make intelligent decisions pertaining to selection of the best countries to enter for marketing their products and/or services (Mitri et al. 1991).

The database of the Country Consultant is organized in terms of four *concept types* (to use the Country Consultant terminology): *feature, industry, entry mode* and *market*. A *feature* is a characteristic of a market/country which enables categorization of the information available on various characteristics of that market/country. Features range from macro categories such as "commercial environment" to micro categories such as "patent protection." *Industry* refers to the product classifications used by the Country Consultant. Again, industries are categorized at different levels of aggregation, such as "consumer goods" (a general category) or "pharmaceutical" (a more specific category). *Entry mode* refers to the different forms of entering a foreign market such as exporting, licensing or joint ventures. *Market* refers to a particular country included in the database. The four concept types are independent of each other and each is structured via a hierarchical arrangement of concepts. This hierarchical structuring of concepts allows the Country Consultant to employ AI techniques for intelligently responding to user queries for market evaluation information. Figure 1 shows a structural description of the Country Consultant, and illustrates the information flow incorporated within.

It is important to point out the criteria used in identifying the concepts included under the concept types and the hierarchies that were developed. The concepts included under the *feature* concept-type and their hierarchical ordering were identified through a thorough review of the theoretical and empirical studies reported in the literature and through consulting experts in the field. In other words, as mentioned before, through this process the information categories identified were mapped onto a feature hierarchy in the

Figure 1

Structural components and information flow of Country Consultant. Judge enters information based on expert knowledge and market research findings. User queries the system for information, which triggers inferencing process. Semantic networks aid in knowledge organization and inferencing.

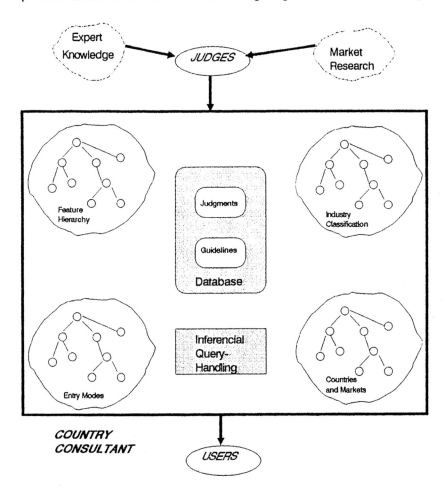

Country Consultant, as discussed in the previous section. Figure 2 shows the main information categories included in the feature concept in the Country Consultant and how they are related to the information categories suggested in the literature. The concepts included under the industry concept-type correspond to the industry classifications suggested by the U.S. Department of Commerce. Various forms of entry to foreign markets are included under the entry mode concept. Finally, markets referring to major trading partners of the U.S. Information in the Country Consultant are stored in *judgment* and *guideline* records. The judgments provide *valuative* information and guidelines provide *descriptive* information pertaining to a particular combination of the above mentioned four concepts. Figure 3 shows an example of a judgment on commercial environment (feature) in Germany (market) for export (entry mode) of medical equipment (industry). As this figure suggests, each judgment (and each guideline) in the Country Consultant is indexed via a combination of a particular feature, industry, entry mode and market. This is called a *concept combination* in the terminology of Country Consultant.

The Country Consultant Infers Unknown Judgments

Obviously, a database with large numbers of industry classes, markets, features and entry modes will have a very large possible number of judgments and/or guidelines. Currently the breakdown of conceptual primitives in the database is as follows: 57 market features; 98 industry categories; 11 entry modes; and 39 markets. This results in 2,396,394 (57 × 98 × 11 × 39) possible judgments in the database. Of course, it is not feasible for experts to enter all of these judgments. This is especially true because we are forcing judgments to be well-researched, and well-supported, with citations to government, academic, and industry publications. In addition, the volatility of market research information requires that the database be updated continuously, which makes it doubly difficult to comprehensively store all possible information. Therefore, the Country Consultant should be able to *infer* what a judgment should be upon request, even if that judgment has not been explicitly entered by an expert. This inference is based on the explicit judg-

Figure 2

Relation of features used in the Country Consultant to the information categories suggested in the academic literature.

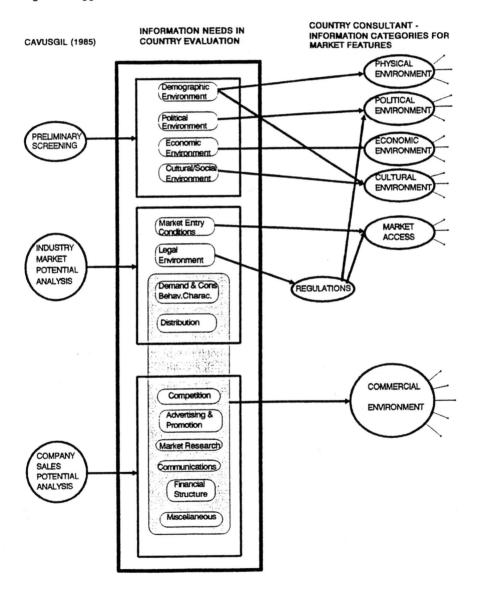

Figure 3

A sample judgment entry screen.

Current Feature is:	Commercial Environment	Judgment Date
Current Industry is:	Medical Equipment	3-July-1991
Current Mode is:	GENERAL	
Current Market is:	Germany	

Judgment

Excellent
Good
Fair
Poor
Terrible

Direction

Rapidly Improving
Improving
Stable
Deteriorating
Rapidly Deteriorating

Judgment Confidence

0.80

Direction Confidence

0.80

Enter your comments here:

U.S. made health care and medical devices are highly regarded in Germany. This area offers large sales and growth opportunities. (Business America, March 1991)

ments that are "conceptually close" to it. Conceptual closeness is determined by the relative positions of a judgment's concept combination in the feature, industry, and entry mode hierarchies. Additionally, with such a large database, it is important to maintain the integrity of the content of the database. Judgments should be consistent with each other. Thus, the Country Consultant's inferencing mechanism serves to "second-guess" the judges who enter information.

The method used to infer in the Country Consultant combines techniques from AI with ideas from multi-attribute utility theory (MAUT). The database is indexed via a *semantic network,* which underlies the structure of the markets, industries, features, and entry modes. This allows the use of *spreading activation,* by which the system can search for concepts that are related to the user's query. In inferring a judgment, the Country Consultant uses a *linear weighted model* to combine the judgments found via spreading activation. Each judgment's weight of influence is based on its conceptual closeness to the query judgment and on the confidence level assigned to the judgment.[4]

Hence, in addition to serving as a repository of processed, judgmental knowledge, the Country Consultant also has the facility to respond intelligently to queries made by the user. If it cannot find a judgment that specifically meets the user's query, it can infer a likely value for that judgment by searching the database for conceptually similar judgments. Moreover, it can provide a "second guess" for the evaluation of a concept combination if a judgment has already been entered.

Validation of Information in the Country Consultant

The validation process for Country Consultant is sequential and dynamic in nature. It consists of three stages for internal and external validation of the system.

The first stage focuses on initial screening and structural development of Country Consultant. Here information entered by students and researchers is screened for qualitative errors and concept combinations. The second stage focuses on expert opinion–qualitative testing where Country Consultant is put through a rigorous in-house testing process. In this phase, internal consistency of information and its reliability is tested. The third stage consists of validation coupled with expert opinion (for detailed information on this process, please refer to Evirgen et al. 1992).

EXPERIENCES USING THE COUNTRY CONSULTANT IN THE CLASSROOM

The Country Consultant has been used as a pedagogical tool for teaching business students techniques of international market research. The following sections describe how it was used in three classroom settings, with undergraduate, masters, and doctorate students.

There are two main motivations for our use of Country Consultant in the classroom. One reason is to make use of the student body to aid in collecting the information to put into the database. The second is to provide an alternative method of teaching students how to do research in the area of international marketing. An advantage of using the database is that it imposes a structure on the student's research activity that is not normally found in other class projects such as term papers. Because the information in the Country Consultant is categorized according to market feature, industry classification, and entry mode, this provides a framework for students to use in their research effort. In short, imposing such a structure helps to focus the student by giving him or her an idea of what it is s/he is looking for.

The sections below discuss how the Country Consultant was used in classroom settings for the past two years. The method of using the country consultant was also changed over the different terms. In addition, Figure 4 shows a flow chart of the general methodology for Country Consultant's use as a pedagogical tool.

Early Use: Graduate Level

We first used Country Consultant in Winter term 1991. In this graduate-level international marketing class, the students were given an option to aid in the market research and data entry into the Country Consultant in lieu of doing a term paper. Fourteen students chose this option. Students had the option of working alone or with a partner. Each student (or team) selected a country to research. The countries included France, India, Ireland, Israel, Japan, Malaysia, Singapore, South Africa, and Germany.

Each student's assignment was to gather secondary information about the country she/he was working on pertaining to the various features, industry classifications, and entry modes of the Country Consultant. Students were expected to gather this information from government documents (such as U.S. Department of Commerce Country Market Plans), trade journals and periodicals (such as Business International, Price Waterhouse, or Dun and Bradstreet reports), academic literature, or any other timely and reliable sources they could find.

In addition to gathering information about the market, the stu-

Figure 4

General methodology for using Country Consultant in the classroom.

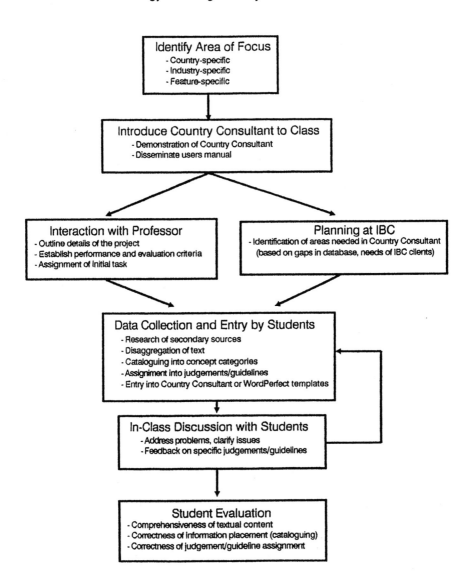

dents were required to thoroughly analyze the information. Specifically, they needed to classify it according to the appropriate feature, industry, and entry mode. This involved extracting paragraphs, sentences, or phrases from the literature, then segregating and categorizing these text fragments. This was perhaps the most challenging and time-consuming aspect of the assignment. It required the student to do a sort of *content analysis* of the text, and to really understand what the text was saying.

After categorizing the text, they needed to decide whether that text related to judgmental information (i.e., an evaluative statement of good or bad, improving or deteriorating) or merely descriptive, guideline information. If it was judgmental information, the student was expected to assign a judgment (excellent, good, fair, poor, or terrible) and direction (rapidly improving, improving, stable, deteriorating, or rapidly deteriorating). In addition, the students were expected to give a confidence level for the judgment and direction, indicating how secure they felt that the text obtained actually supports the judgment and direction assigned (see Figure 3 for a sample judgment).

Finally, after collecting, disaggregating, classifying, and assigning judgments to the market research information, students were required to enter the information directly into the Country Consultant. Thus, these students got hands-on experience in directly using the software.

Later Use: Graduate and Undergraduate

As a result of the initial positive experience with using the Country Consultant in the classroom, we repeated this process on a larger scale in Fall term 1991. However, because of the increased volume of students involved, and because we were not prepared to make many copies of the Country Consultant or to provide network access, it was not feasible to have students directly enter the data using the Country Consultant. Instead, each student was supplied with a floppy disk containing two ASCII text files, called JUDGE and GUIDE. These files were "templates" in which to fill judgment or guideline information. The students could use any word processor to fill in this information, provided that they saved the files as

ASCII text files. Then, the students would turn in their floppy disks, and a computer program would automatically enter the information into the Country Consultant's database.

Another difference between the earlier class and the later classes is the focus of their research. In the earlier class, the students were assigned a *country* to study. By contrast, in later classes each student (or team) was assigned an *industry,* and was to study this industry across several markets. The industries assigned were computers and peripherals, computer software and services, medical and health care equipment, telecommunications equipment, electronic equipment, pollution control equipment, automotive parts and accessories, analytical laboratory and scientific equipment, machine tools, and food processing and packaging equipment. These industries were selected because they were rated as the highest demand industries by the U.S. Department of Commerce Country Market Plans.

Our reason for the change of focus was that the initial data collection had resulted in a rich set of information for macro-indicators (economic environment, political stability, etc.), but rather sparse information pertaining to industry-specific micro-indicators. The need for gathering industry-specific information was a prime motivation for changing the focus of the data collection assignment.

Other than these two differences, data collection and analysis processes of the students, and our evaluation process were the same in both sets of classes.

Evaluation of Students

The students were evaluated according to several criteria. The quantity of judgments and guidelines entered for the country was one indicator. They were also graded based on the comprehensiveness of the information they entered. In other words, were they covering many bases or just concentrating on a few features of the market? The accuracy of information classification was also a major indicator. For example, if the text pertained to tariffs or duties and the user assigned it to a GENERAL feature or to a Commercial Environment feature, this would be an incorrect classification (too general) and would lower their overall grade. In this way, we were able to evaluate the student's comprehension of the material s/he had read. Improper classification is an indicator that the student did not really understand the material, or that s/he did not understand important issues in international marketing that were being covered in the class. We also graded based on the number and quality of the sources used. For example, if a judgment's text cited several credible sources this would indicate that the quality of the judgment would be better than a judgment citing only a single source. Based on our evaluation of the content and placement of judgments and guidelines, the researchers at IBC made modifications to the entered data, thus making it usable for IBC's counselling requirements.

Contributions to Student's Learning

The students' experience with the Country Consultant has contributed to their learning of international marketing in various ways. First of all, the hierarchical structures of the concepts in the Country Consultant represent a consolidation and integration of previous models cited in the literature. Although the industry and entry mode hierarchies are pretty self-evident, the feature hierarchy is not so. In the literature, different models/frameworks have been suggested for information requirements in foreign market evaluation, but no one single model/framework has incorporated all of the points raised. The feature hierarchy in the Country Consultant presents a cohesive and integrated framework for information requirements in foreign market evaluation. Through working with the Country Consultant, the students had the opportunity to learn about the information categories and their subcategories that are important in evaluating foreign markets.

Secondly, the students had the opportunity to learn about the important features of the countries they worked on. Since they had to find information about the countries related to the features included in the feature hierarchy, they were able to analyze foreign markets in terms of the relevant criteria. This of course helped the students to broaden their knowledge of world markets.

Thirdly, their experience with the Country Consultant helped the students to learn how to conduct research in international marketing. The students had to find the required information to make judgments through researching secondary sources. Through this research process, they learned about the different types of secondary sources available on foreign market characteristics and about the type of information and/or data contained in each. After having gone through their experience with the Country Consultant, they had a better understanding of desk research in international marketing and how to go about doing that type of research.

Fourth, the Country Consultant imposed a structure on the research activities of the students through the hierarchical structures of its concepts. The students had to find information on concept combinations formed by a given set of features, industries and entry modes. Thus, they knew exactly what to look for, which considerably facilitated their research activities. They were, in fact, guided by the structure of the Country Consultant. This is very important, especially in the area of international market information. The reason is that there is a vast amount of dispersed and at times diverse information on foreign markets. Hence, unless one follows a well-structured research process, it is very easy to be overwhelmed with the information, not knowing what to do with it.

Fifth, the students had an exposure to artificial intelligence and its use in international marketing. Although decision support systems are finding more and more appeal in the business world, applications of such systems in international marketing are still rare. Having worked with such a system will be a valuable asset for these students, especially when they graduate and look for a job.

Sixth, the students also were able to contribute to an ongoing research. This also increased their satisfaction with their experience with the Country Consultant. Most of their input was actually put into actual use after a careful examination by the research staff at IBC.

Finally, all of the students were even more interested in international marketing after their experience with the Country Consultant. This project increased their enthusiasm about international marketing issues.

We found the use of the Country Consultant in the classroom was a positive experience for the students as well as an aid for our overall intelligent database project. Comments from the students indicated that they found the experience very worthwhile and an enjoyable change-of-pace from the normal "write a term paper" kind of class project. They typically found the structure of the Country Consultant to be helpful in guiding their own research. They also expressed satisfaction since the work they had done was actually going to be used to help future users of the Country Consultant. This is another way in which entering their market research into a database is an improvement over writing a term paper.

In addition, the students were able to make suggestions on how to improve the quality of the software itself, by making it more user friendly and by adding to or modifying the list of features and industry categories. As a result of their input, we made several enhancements to the program.

CONCLUSIONS

In this article, we have attempted to achieve a number of objectives. First, the information requirements framework suggested here is an attempt to present a coherent and integrative framework based on the previous literature bringing together different frameworks and suggestions. This framework can be used by researchers in this area in the future as a common starting point.

Secondly, the decision support tool described here, namely the Country Consultant, is a unique application of AI techniques to the field of international marketing. Such an "intelligent" system whose "intelligence" arises from its inferencing capabilities when explicit information is scarce or not available (just as an expert would do) is highly likely to be beneficial for anyone (including both academicians, market researchers, and managers or executives) who needs reliable, relevant and timely information on foreign markets. Furthermore, what makes the Country Consultant unique is that it contains processed, catalogued, judgmental information rather than raw data. "In addition, it uses an indexing schema that accounts for the various models cited in the literature" (Mitri et al., 1991, p. 31).

Third, experiences with using the Country Consultant in the classroom have been very rewarding especially for the students. Through these experiences, we were able to generate significant interest in international marketing. The students were able to

develop their secondary research skills and improve their understanding of foreign markets.

In short, the Country Consultant is a unique application of artificial intelligence techniques to international marketing regarding
information needs in foreign market evaluation. Using this tool in
the classroom as a teaching instrument further adds to its uniqueness. Our experiences with using such a system in the classroom
show that intelligent databases can be very effective tools to facilitate the learning process of the students.[5]

NOTES

1. IBC is comprised of two units. The Center for International Business Education and Research (CIBER) is one of sixteen national resource centers funded by
the U.S. Department of Education. Development of Country Consultant and other
expert systems is taking place at CIBER as part of its research activities. The
Michigan International Business Development Center (MI-IBDC) provides counselling and assistance in internationalization and export planning to small and
medium-sized companies in Michigan.

2. This section is adapted from Mitri et al. (1991).

3. See Mitri et al. (1991) for a more detailed description of the Country
Consultant.

4. A detailed description of the inference method used by Country Consultant,
as well as a review of semantic networks and their use in databases, can be found
in chapter 7 of Mitri (1992).

5. The Country Consultant is currently being used and validated in-house at
IBC. We intend to make the software commercially available late in 1992. For
more information, contact: International Business Centers, 6 Kellogg Center,
Michigan State University, East Lansing, MI 48824-1022; or call (517)
353-4336.

REFERENCES

Bodur, Muzaffer & Cavusgil, S. Tamer (1984). Export Market Research Orientations of Turkish Firms. *European Journal of Marketing,* 19:2, 5-16.

Bodur, Muzaffer (1986). A Study on the Nature and Intensity of Problems Experienced by Turkish Exporting Firms. In S. Tamer Cavusgil (ed). *Advances in
International Marketing,* Vol. 1, Greenwich, CT: JAI Press, Inc., 205-231.

Brodie, M.L. (1988). Future Intelligent Information Systems: AI and Database
Technologies Working Together. In Mylopolopus and Brodie (ed). *Readings in
Artificial Intelligence and Databases.* Morgan Kaufmann Publishers, Inc.,
623-642.

Cavusgil, S. Tamer & Nevin, John R. (1983). *International Marketing: An Annotated Bibliography*, Chicago, IL:AMA.

Cavusgil, S. Tamer (1984a). Differences Among Exporting Firms Based on Their Degree of Internationalization. *Journal of Business Research*, 12:2, 195-208.

Cavusgil, S. Tamer (1984b). International Marketing Research: Insights into Company Practices. *Research in Marketing*, 7, 261-288.

Cavusgil, S. Tamer (1985). Guidelines for Export Market Research. *Business Horizons*, Nov/Dec.

Cavusgil, S. Tamer (1987). Qualitative Insights into Company Experiences in International Marketing Research. *The Journal of Business & Industrial Marketing*, Summer, 41-54.

Daser, Sayeste (1985). International Marketing Information Systems: A Neglected Prerequisite for Foreign Marketing Planning. In *Global Perspectives in Marketing*, Erdener Kaynak, ed., NY: Praeger Publishers, 139-153.

Davidson, William H. (1983). Marketing Similarities and Market Selection: Implications for International Marketing Strategy. *Journal of Business Research*, 11 (December), 439-456.

Douglas, Susan & C. Samuel Craig (1988). Information for International Marketing Decisions. In Ingo Walter and Tracy Murray, (eds.), *Handbook of International Business*. New York: John Wiley & Sons, 29.3-29.33.

Ehrman, Chaim Meyer & Morris Hamburg (1986). Information Search for Foreign Direct Investment Using Two-Stage Country Selection Procedures: A New Procedure. *Journal of International Business Studies*, Summer, 83-88.

Evirgen, Cuneyt (1990). Information Need Assessment for Exporters. *Unpublished Master's thesis*, Bosphorous University, Istanbul, Turkey.

Evirgen, Cuneyt (1992). A Causal Model for Foreign Market Attractiveness and Use of an Expert System as the Knowledge Base. Accepted for publication in *Proceedings of the AMA 1992 Summer Educator's Conference (forthcoming)*.

Evirgen, Cuneyt & Bhargava, Vivek & Mitri, Mike & Cavusgil, S. Tamer (1992). A Sequential And Dynamic Testing Methodology For Validating An Expert System Application. Accepted for publication in *Proceedings of the AMA 1992 Summer Educator's Conference (forthcoming)*.

Frisch, A. & Allen, J. (1988). Knowledge Retrieval as Limited Inference. In Mylopolopus and Brodie (eds.), *Readings in Artificial Intelligence and Databases*. Morgan Kaufmann Publishers, Inc. 1988. pp. 444-451.

Hutcheson, J.M. (1984). International Marketing Techniques for Engineers. *International Marketing Review*, Autumn/Winter, 51-59.

Jobber, D. (1982). International Marketing Research–Effective Use of Secondary Sources. *Industrial Management+ DataSystems*, Sept/Oct, 18-21.

Johanson, Jan & Jan-Erik Vahlne (1977). The Internationalization of the Firm–A Model of Knowledge Development and Increasing Foreign market Commitments. *Journal of International Business Studies*, Spring/Summer, 23-31.

Kahler, Ruel (1983). *International Marketing*, USA: South-Western Publ. Co., USA.

Keegan, Warren J. (1989). *Global Marketing Management,* Englewood Cliffs, NJ: Prentice-Hall, Inc..

Keng, Kau Ah & Jivan, Tan Soo. (1989). Differences Between Small and Medium-sized Exporting and Non-exporting Firms: Nature or Nurture. *International Marketing Review,* 6:4, 27-40.

Mitri, Mike, Cuneyt Evirgen & S. Tamer Cavusgil (1991). The Country Consultant: An Expert System for the International Marketing Executive. *Proceedings of the 1991 AMA Microcomputers on the Marketing Education Conference,* (August), 21-33.

Mitri, Michel (1992). Candidate Evaluation: a Task Specific Architecture using Multiattribute Utility Theory with Applications in International Marketing. *Unpublished PhD Dissertation.* Computer Science Department. Michigan State University.

Staudt, Thomas A., Donald A. Taylor, & Donald J. Bowersox (1976). *A Managerial Introduction to Marketing,* Englewood Cliffs, NJ: Prentice-Hall, Inc. 1976.

Trip, Johan F. Laman (1985). International Research Needs Downstream Pioneering. *European Research,* July, 97-108.

Walters, Peter G.P. (1983). Export Information Sources–A Study of Their Usage and Utility. *International Marketing Review,* Winter, 34-43.

Wood, Van R. & Jerry R. Goolsby (1987). Foreign Market Information Preferences of Established U.S. Exporters. *International Marketing Review,* Winter, 43-52.

An Early Critical Examination of Using Simulation in the Teaching of International Marketing: An Evaluation of "Export To Win!"

George V. Priovolos

SUMMARY. An export marketing simulation game, "Export To Win!", is evaluated for its pedagogical contribution to an undergraduate international marketing course. Criteria used in the evaluation include instructional, usage, and presentation characteristics, user control, and students' personal/professional development. On the basis of the observed strengths and weaknesses in the use of ETW, the paper offers several suggestions for designing and implementing similar programs in the future.

INTRODUCTION

Despite the increased attention that international business studies are receiving in U.S. higher education, little has changed with

George V. Priovolos, PhD, is associated with the Department of Marketing, Hagan School of Business, Iona College, 715 North Avenue, New Rochelle, NY 10801.

[Haworth co-indexing entry note]: "An Early Critical Examination of Using Simulation in the Teaching of International Marketing: An Evaluation of "Export To Win!"" Priovolos, George V. Co-published simultaneously in the *Journal of Teaching in International Business* (The Haworth Press, Inc.) Vol. 4, No. 3/4, 1993, pp. 39-54; and: *Utilizing New Information Technology in Teaching of International Business: A Guide for Instructors* (ed: Fahri Karakaya and Erdener Kaynak) The Haworth Press, Inc., 1993, pp. 39-54. Multiple copies of this article/chapter may be purchased from The Haworth Document Delivery Center. Call 1-800-3-HA-WORTH (1-800-342-9678) between 9:00 - 5:00 (EST) and ask for DOCUMENT DELIVERY CENTER.

39

regard to the methods used in teaching these subjects. That is bound to change with the development and adoption of computer software whose purpose is to supplement, expand, and enrich international business curricula. Specifically, in the teaching of international marketing, the use of computers may help by both disseminating knowledge and sharpening student perceptual as well as decision-making skills. Moreover, appropriate software could motivate students to learn and develop the necessary attitudes vis-à-vis the ever-increasing globalization of business. Instructors also should benefit from computerizing their international business courses by acquiring novel global insights/perspectives and having an opportunity to rethink and possibly redesign their pedagogical approach.

With this in mind, the present paper, drawing on the experience of the author from introducing "EXPORT TO WIN!" (ETW) to a selected group of undergraduate students, (a) briefly describes the software's major features; (b) attempts to attract attention to the potential benefits/problems arising from its use in the teaching of an undergraduate international marketing course, and (c) suggests a number of desirable features that should be incorporated into international marketing educational software in the future.

A critical examination of the issues involved in the computerization of international marketing studies is deliberately conducted at this early stage in the process as a preventive measure: pedagogical "traps" can and should be identified as early as possible to avoid the waste inherent in a "trial and error" approach and prevent any potential negative impact on a whole generation of students.

A BRIEF DESCRIPTION OF "EXPORT TO WIN!"

ETW, a software program originally developed by SMG Strategic Management Group, Inc. in association with the Port Authority of NY/NJ to introduce small businessmen to the practices of export marketing, has been recently made available in a student edition. According to the publisher, ETW is a "highly interactive . . . instructional business program designed to help (the student) understand the exporting process better."

In brief, the program places the student in the position of the marketing manager of Xebec, an industrial manufacturer of two main products–a fully-assembled process control unit and process control components, who must develop an export plan for them. His/her given goal is to turn the company into a successful global competitor; by analyzing target markets, putting together an effective distribution network, and negotiating international pricing, the student/manager is expected to achieve a pre-determined goal (at least $6 million in export revenues) by the end of five simulation years. To help him/her in making the required decisions, the program provides strategy suggestions and other on-screen information as well as directions on how to obtain additional relevant research and resources.

To provide the unfamiliar reader with a flavor of the program, Appendix A of this paper depicts the flow of events and decisions that an EWT player would face in the "first year of operations." Simulations of export activities in successive years follow a similar structure although decision-making topics change. The program requires PC-DOS/MS-DOS 2.0 or higher, at least 640K RAM, 2 disk drives (and/or a hard disk), and a color graphics card.

EVALUATION OF "EXPORT TO WIN!"

An intensive qualitative analysis of ETW's features was undertaken to assess its fitness and usefulness in the teaching of international marketing. Papers dealing with the use of computers in classroom curricula usually refer to the ways in which software can be used in teaching a course, the potential pedagogical benefits derived from it, and the various requirements (hardware, students' computer literacy, etc.) for such usage. In addition to the issues above, software reviews should raise questions concerning the limits of computer-aided instruction by means of the specific program (i.e., what the software in question *cannot* do) as well as questions about the role that computers and computer software can play in the personal, professional, and social development of students (Ellison 1989; Bohland and Anderson 1978).

In view of this, ETW was analyzed by the author in terms of its instructional, usage, and presentation characteristics, the amount of user control it allows, and its other contributions towards student development. Notes from observations of a small group of 12 students, who used the software on an experimental basis over the course of two semesters, were consulted for this analysis. A sense of student appreciation of the software was also obtained by examining their answers to several questions about the program's features, usefulness, and recommendations for improvement (see Appendix B for a copy of the Student Software Evaluation Form used for this purpose).

Admittedly, the present group of students and the environment in which they experienced the simulation game do not represent a realistic and typical implementation of the software in the teaching of international marketing; they instead provide an early "case study" which was analyzed to appraise the program's capabilities, identify its strengths and weaknesses and suggest steps for the successful development of other international marketing/business educational software in the future.

Instructional Characteristics

The contribution of computer software in the curriculum may vary depending on the intensity of its use as well as the role which it is assigned in the teaching of international marketing. For instance, computers may be used occasionally as a resource facility much like a library (only more readily accessible). Alternatively, they may be used regularly in the course to augment learning through the presentation of supplemental materials and development of special skills or as *the* instructor, largely independent of student exposure to human teachers (Lehman, Starr and Young 1978). ETW sets the following *three learning objectives* for its student-users: (a) learn that exporting makes good business sense; (b) learn about the importance of research and developing an international marketing plan, and (c) discover how proper export management will permit global marketing ("Export To Win!" Student Guide 1991, p. vi). Overall, the program seems to accomplish these objectives and is particularly effective in stressing the importance of conducting thorough on-going market research for achieving success in international marketing.

Unfortunately, in contrast to its stated learning objectives, ETW has been positioned as a simulation game teaching "good global business practices"–which it is not! Computers when used as simulators allow students to explore the basic concepts/hypotheses in international marketing and examine policy decisions in terms of their feasibility/consequences *by doing*. Simulations duplicate the essential characteristics of a system or activity; they serve to demonstrate behavior and explain it in terms of the various functional relationships contained in a system (including any exogenous constraints) (Calkins 1978). For instance, international marketing instructors may teach students the important factors influencing a company's international pricing decision by placing them in the position of the decision-maker (i.e., marketing manager), ask them to determine price and then let them see the results of their decision on the financial statements of the company. Unfortunately, the small number of decisions required by ETW and the narrow range of available options as well as the lack of immediate and discernible results that the student can directly attribute to his/her choices may be counterproductive. There is especially a need for improvement in the way the program communicates to the student the results of his/her performance. For instance, calculations of how individual choices contribute to better/worse financial performance (also a measure of a student's performance in the game) should be shown in more detail while an on-screen Print option can give the student (and the instructor) a permanent record of his/her performance.

ETW was designed as a *practical training tool*; although some student-users may learn a few new cognitive skills, particularly the step-by-step approach to problem-solving, this program does not make any demands on its users' ability for critical thinking. The latter is evident when, for example, research sources and findings are cited throughout the simulation without any attempt to evaluate their reliability or question their quality. Students are led to either accept this information unquestionably or base their acceptance on cost considerations alone. It is thus left to the international marketing instructor to emphasize the quality of information rather than its cost in his/her classroom presentations (for a discussion of the quality/cost trade-off in export marketing research see, for example, Kothari 1983).

The program provides some positive reinforcement in the form of verbal rewards for the user's correct decisions (e.g., when s/he chooses to learn more about the competition as opposed to proceeding without such information). Further positive reinforcement is offered at the end of each year when the student views the financial and operational results of his/her decisions and at the end of the game with the accomplishment of the initial goal of $6 million in export revenues. Moreover, ETW handles incorrect decisions in a constructive manner–after explaining the reasons why the choice is mistaken, it offers the student the opportunity to reconsider and make another choice (Figure 1).

Usage Characteristics

Students who had an opportunity to use ETW reported that they needed very little preparation for learning the program. Once they familiarized themselves with the basic workings of the game and the specific functions that the special keys (F1 through F6) perform by reading the manual, they were able to run the program without any particular difficulty. However, instructors may need to become well acquainted with ETW's structure and especially its length in

FIGURE 1

You have definitely made a fatal error.

A basic rule in business is to know your competition and this principle applies to exporting as well as your other business activities.

Do you want to reconsider your decision?

Press Escape if you want to reconsider, RETURN if you really want to export in the dark.

order to determine the depth/width of knowledge that they wish their students to acquire in each session. Since ETW's strength, as already mentioned, is in dealing with practical rather than conceptual issues, instructors should realize that they will need additional time in the classroom to introduce the student to the theory of international marketing themselves. Extra time should also be devoted to informing students about current international business developments and comparing the latter to the sometimes outdated information contained in ETW (as well as their textbook) (e.g., the political environment in the ex-U.S.S.R. or the movement of the European Community towards political and monetary integration).

It is highly unlikely that a whole year's run of the program can fit within the usual 55-75-minute undergraduate class. Thus, instructors may urge students to either complete only 2-3 of a year's "event clusters" and save their place in the simulation for another session or postpone obtaining on-screen information about some words/phrases which will be encountered again in future sessions. The use of the student guide that includes a glossary defining important terms found in the program and a resources and references section along with a variety of learning exercises, if properly incorporated into the course, can help make the game more manageable and enjoyable for both instructor and student.

Probably, one of the most disappointing features of ETW is its atomistic orientation. Although the student assumes the role of a marketing manager in a fictitious company, his/her only contact with "others" throughout the game is in the form of a few memos that s/he receives from the company's CEO. The fact that there is no provision in the program for accommodating multiple players may be detrimental to its ability to achieve important instructional, motivational and/or personal development goals. To the extent that the real-world of international business is characterized by team work and joint decision-making, the program misses the opportunity to develop such desired skills as the ability to deal with the problems of effectively organizing a group to undertake complex decision-making.

Presentation Characteristics

International marketers employ various language forms in their descriptions and analyses: numeric symbols, spoken and/or written words, and graphic presentations. Therefore, good international marketing software should communicate with its users by means of all three language forms. ETW appears to be text-dominated with few notable exceptions (e.g., diagramatic explanation of flow of goods and funds between seller and buyer under different credit arrangements). More extensive use of graphics would certainly improve overall presentation and increase student attention and interest. As is, ETW's almost exclusive reliance on text may, on the one hand, be appealing to a substantial number of international marketing students who are not mathematically inclined; however, on the other hand, to the degree that quantification helps attain accuracy and rigor in thinking and expression, the program may confuse users' understanding (and attainment) of satisfactory results. ETW uses color well, e.g., to distinguish between event clusters whose decisions have been made from those still undecided.

User Control

ETW enhances user control by providing some branching alternatives, allowing the student to save a current session into a designated file and re-load it at a later time, and offering a summary of each year's issues for quick reference. In addition, ETW allows users to proceed at their own speed, a feature particularly liked by students who used it in this study. Instructors, though, may wish to exercise some control over the game's pace by imposing a series of semi-threatening deadlines to avoid potential student procrastination and falling behind. Although, at times, ETW gives the student/ user a sense of control by empowering him/her to make certain marketing decisions especially in choosing how much and what kind of information s/he will obtain before proceeding to make these decisions, the computer appears to remain firmly in control throughout the program's run. Students, who had an opportunity to use the software, expressed particular dissatisfaction with the limited range of options available to them for each decision. In some cases, they felt the alternatives offered were "naive" and "unintelligent." An example repeatedly cited in this regard was the "choice" to obtain more information about exporting or not (claiming that you–the user–know(s) enough already (see Figure 2a);

Figure 2b shows a more sophisticated choice in ETW). Other ETW features that produced confusion and frustration were: the imposition of predetermined objectives (generating $6 million in export revenues within the 5-year period), the inability to play directly against competition, the need to re-enter an event cluster in order to change decisions (in only a few cases, the program offered the opportunity to change selection by using the Esc key), the limited opportunity for navigating through the program non-sequentially (i.e., students deciding themselves what question they should answer next), and the long lists of seemingly unrelated points that the program advises players "to keep under consideration" (see Figure 3 for an example of one such list appearing under "control" in the discussion of different market entry strategies).

Student Development

Most International Business software like ETW should encourage student discovery both for its intrinsic value as well as the enthusiasm about the program that it generates. Discovery, of course, requires a willingness on the part of a student to stretch his/her limits of competence. A number of international marketing undergraduate students who possess it may still be prevented from being creative by their reluctance to accept the possibility of failure in a traditional classroom setting. It appears that ETW may provide

FIGURE 2a

Would you like more information about steps to take in learning more about exporting?

1. Yes, I want to get started

2. No, I feel I know enough already

Select a number to make a decision

FIGURE 2b

DIRECT EXPORTING

You can export directly through one of the
following:

		Mark-up range as a % of Export Sales
1.	Agent	3%-15%
2.	Distributor	10%-50%
3.	Agent & Distributor	

Select a number to decide on a direct
exporting medium or a letter to obtain more
information.

Compare the two methods

A Business Brief

How do you find an agent/distributor?

(Esc. to previous screen)

an excellent one-on-one environment that would facilitate the pursuit of learning new ideas and practices.

Furthermore, ETW helps in promoting students' personal/professional development in a number of ways, which are particularly important for future international marketing managers. For instance, the simulation by its construction (5-year horizon) teaches students to employ longer time frames in their marketing decision-making. Moreover, through its emphasis on information gathering

FIGURE 3

CONTROL

Keep the following under consideration:

- Your personnel

- Pricing

- Marketing Strategies

- Sales Techniques

- Delivery

- Installation

- After sales service

- Spare parts

- Confidential information,
  patents, trademarks

and analysis, it develops student appreciation of the complexity of policy-makers' problems and the necessity of closely monitoring environmental trends.

ETW is also successful in its efforts to educate students/users about cultural differences and how they impact decision-making and individual behavior in general. Students using ETW especially liked the concise, but information-packed, country profiles on England, France, Germany, and Japan and the tips on their respective customs/lifestyles. Nevertheless, in a subtle way, the program may be adopting an ethnocentric approach to globalization! This oxymoron derives directly from some of the game's main characteristics—many of them undoubtedly designed to simplify the internationalization process and adapt the game to user needs: insistence on the outmoded dichotomy between "ours" (U.S. company/product) and "theirs" (foreign companies/products) (Reich 1991); emphasis on differences between countries/markets as opposed to similarities, and the implicit assumption that international marketing experiences and strategies are totally different from domestic ones (companies have to deal with significant cultural, economic, and other diversity *within* the U.S., too).

Overall, though, this program approaches international marketing in the way the manager of a medium-sized firm should do, starting with a limited knowledge of the particulars of international commerce but gradually advancing his/her sophistication in tandem with his/her global market involvement. Once students have been exposed to these marketplace realities, they are better prepared to undergo the mental and emotional adjustments needed in their future professional careers.

CONCLUSION

We are now in the introductory stage of the computerization of undergraduate international marketing/business curricula. As an early entry on the market for international marketing/business software, ETW, the particular program evaluated in this paper, is likely to attract instructors eager to computerize their courses. Undoubtedly, use of this program in an international marketing course will significantly enhance the effectiveness of more traditional means of instruction (lectures, cases, videos, field trips, etc.) and benefit students by: (a) giving them the opportunity to experience the way international business takes place; (b) providing students with a wealth of practical information about how to engage themselves in international marketing; (c) helping them understand export marketing practices and the, often confusing, terms used in the trade, and (d) teaching students to strive for internationalization, pursue such a course through proper marketing planning, and always keep themselves in touch with changing environmental trends.

This paper also examined some of the weaknesses of ETW in order to draw ideas and suggestions for designing and implementing better computer software for teaching international marketing in the future. On the basis of this study's findings regarding the use of

ETW, those with a stake in the computerization of the international marketing curriculum (instructors, software developers, publishers, etc.) should adopt/develop software that:

- allow students to *work as groups* rather than as individuals to foster cooperation and mutual support.
- provide *user freedom and flexibility* by allowing him/her to move at variable speeds and letting them "revisit" decisions whenever their initial choice was wrong.
- give *immediate and meaningful feedback* that balances, on the one hand, the need for positive rewards and constructive criticism and, on the other, student desire for clarity, fairness, recognition, and competitiveness.
- are *accessible* to even those international marketing students who have little computer background but without becoming electronic versions of the course textbook.
- are highly *adaptable and flexible* in terms of their input, transformation processes, and responses to avoid becoming obsolete and/or irrelevant as environmental conditions change.
- are perceived as new, unique, and exciting by students; hence, the need for *innovative use of graphics, animation, color, and sound effects.*
- address instructors' needs for *better documentation* including suggestions for curricular implementation, tips for student motivation, and innovative applications.

A course preparing students for careers in international marketing in the 21st century would require *both widespread adoption of computer technology as well as revision of current curriculum content.* International marketing software teaching students how to place international business developments within a concrete conceptual perspective and helping them understand the interrelations between the innumerable variables affecting international marketing outcomes will be an indispensable instructional tool in the future. These programs should evolve from focusing primarily on how U.S. corporations may adapt to the internationalization of the marketplace towards viewing U.S. marketing in the *context of world (global) marketing.* More attention to world geography and history to discourage/eliminate any potential western bias will add to the usefulness of such programs. Additionally, future international marketing software should make students aware of such worldwide concerns as energy shortages, overpopulation, economic underdevelopment, and environmental deterioration and their potential impact on international marketing/business. They should also examine the future possibilities for international trade conflict/ cooperation with references to international agreements like the GATT and the emergence of trade blocs. Future international marketing students will be living in a pluralistic global system and be exposed to multiple information sources, each one of them offering a unique world perspective. They will therefore need to learn how to properly analyze, evaluate, and translate this information into appropriate managerial action. Thus, future international marketing educational software must be designed to help in the learning of critical thinking and viewing skills. It should also permit the input of external data (e.g., additional international marketing terms or new environmental parameters) by the instructor or the student.

REFERENCES

Bohland, J.R. and R.E. Anderson, "Computer Literacy" in *Computer Science in Social and Behavioral Science Education,* ed. D.E. Bailey. New Jersey: Educational Technology Publications, Inc., 1978.

Calkins, R.N., "Simulation and the Possibilities of Learning: An Interpretation of the Uses of a Small Computer in Undergraduate Instruction in Economics" in *Computer Science in Social and Behavioral Science Education,* ed. D.E. Bailey. New Jersey: Educational Technology Publications, Inc., 1978.

Ellison, Carol (1989), "PCs in the Schools: An American Tragedy," *PC Computing* (January) 97-104.

"Export To Win!"–Student Edition (1991), *Student Manual,* South-Western Publishing Co.

Hottois, J.W. and S.H. Rakoff, "A Case for Computer Modeling in the Political Science Classroom" in *Computer Science in Social and Behavioral Science Education,* ed. D.E. Bailey. New Jersey: Educational Technology Publications, Inc., 1978.

Kothari, V., "Researching for Export Marketing" in *Export Promotion: The Public and Private Sector Interaction,* ed. M. Czinkota. New York: Praeger Publishers, 1983.

Lehman, R.S., B.J. Starr, and K.C. Young, "Computer Aids in Teaching Statistics and Methodology" in *Computer Science in Social and Behavioral Science Education,* ed. D.E. Bailey. New Jersey: Educational Technology Publications, Inc., 1978.

Reich, Robert (1991), "The Myth of 'Made in the U.S.A.'," *The Wall Street Journal* (July 5).

APPENDIX A

XEBEC COMPANY

First Year Agenda

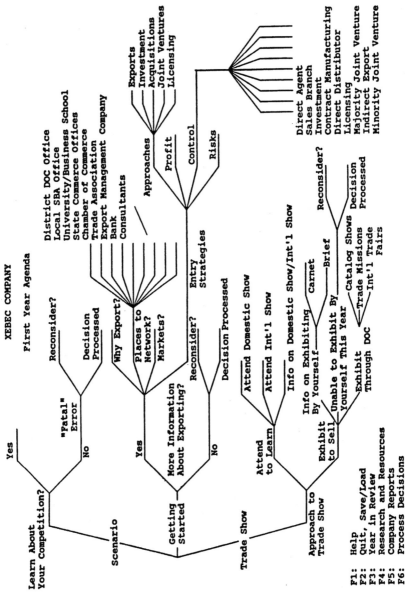

F1: Help
F2: Quit, Save/Load
F3: Year in Review
F4: Research and Resources
F5: Company Reports
F6: Process Decisions

APPENDIX B

STUDENT SOFTWARE EVALUATION FORM

Program Name: **"Export To Win!"**

Student's Name _____

Course & Section _____

How many times have you used this program? _____

On the average, how much time did you spend with the program?
_____

How many years or "event clusters" within a year were you usually able to complete each time that you used the program? _____
_____

Did you need any help using the program? ____ Yes ____ No

What external materials, if any, did you use with this program?
_____

The directions were: ____ good ____ O.K. ____ poor

The graphics were: ____ good ____ O.K. ____ poor

Please comment on the following:

How did the program respond to a wrong answer? _____
_____

How did the program respond to a correct answer? _____
_____

How much in control did you feel using the program? _____
_____

What do you think you accomplished using the program? _____
_____

What did you like best about the program? _____
_____

What did you like the least about the program? _____
_____

What would you like to see changed in this program? _____
_____
_____
_____

Selecting Software
for Teaching International Business:
An Analysis of Existing Programs

Edward W. Schmitt
Gary P. Kearns

SUMMARY. Several software developers have recently introduced very powerful programs designed to assist educators, advisors and businesses to learn more about the exporting process. This paper analyzes the relative strengths and weaknesses of five such programs through the application of international marketing concepts and hypothetical case studies. The analysis herein will save potential users the time and effort needed to select the most appropriate program(s) for their teaching and learning objectives. This paper is intended to address the needs of business program educators and students. It may also be of interest to government agencies and other advisors involved in export education and administration, businesses seeking to learn more about the export-

Edward W. Schmitt, PhD, is Associate Professor in the Department of Marketing at Villanova University, Villanova, PA. Gary P. Kearns is Vice President in Mellon Bank's Corporate Finance Group in Philadelphia, PA.

[Haworth co-indexing entry note]: "Selecting Software for Teaching International Business: An Analysis of Existing Programs." Schmitt, Edward W., and Gary P. Kearns. Co-published simultaneously in the *Journal of Teaching in International Business* (The Haworth Press, Inc.) Vol. 4, No. 3/4, 1993, pp. 55-83; and: *Utilizing New Information Technology in Teaching of International Business: A Guide for Instructors* (ed: Fahri Karakaya and Erdener Kaynak) The Haworth Press, Inc., 1993, pp. 55-83. Multiple copies of this article/chapter may be purchased from The Haworth Document Delivery Center. Call 1-800-3-HAWORTH (1-800-342-9678) between 9:00 - 5:00 (EST) and ask for DOCUMENT DELIVERY CENTER.

55

ing process, and software developers producing programs designed
to teach about exporting.

OVERVIEW

It has been acknowledged in the business, government, and
academic fields that U.S. companies generally have underper-
formed in the exporting arena relative to their European and Asian
counterparts. According to the U.S. Department of Commerce,
only about 15% of all U.S. manufacturers export. Further, the
percentage of the U.S. gross domestic product that comes from
exports is less than 10%, about half the rate of most European
countries. Kefalas (1988) states that a major cause of this sub-par
performance in international trade is a lack of knowledge on the
part of many U.S. businesses about the exporting process. Weber
(1991), supported by many references, argues that college and
university curricula are inadequate in addressing international
business issues.

Surprisingly, this sub-par performance exists despite the U.S.
government's extensive efforts to promote exporting. Part of the
problem has been the inability to effectively package and distribute
to potential users the tremendous volume of information on the
exporting process maintained by public and private sources. Aided
by the increased availability and acceptance of personal computers,
however, several software developers and the federal government
have recently introduced programs which are highly effective in
organizing and retrieving the massive amounts of information available on the exporting process. This paper analyzes five such software programs with an eye to their utility as teaching tools.

While there are other methods to teach about the exporting process (e.g., cases, videotapes, projects, lectures), software programs
such as those analyzed herein are highly effective in organizing and
retrieving fragmented information to meet the specific needs of
individual users. Further, these programs can be utilized in conjunction with other teaching methods. Readers interested in a more
detailed discussion of issues related to the use of computers and
software in business education should refer to International Council

for Computers in Education (1986) and Karakaya and Karakaya (1989).

METHODOLOGY

Primary research to identify software programs that addressed the exporting process was conducted by contacting over twenty-five governmental and private sector sources actively involved in international trade (see Appendix A for a detailed listing). A program was selected for analysis in this paper if it met two basic criteria: (a) its coverage of the exporting process was sufficiently broad to enable its usage by students or business practitioners as a comprehensive educational or training tool; and (b) the program could be run with a personal computer. Programs which were highly specific in nature concerning a certain aspect of the exporting process (e.g., freight management systems or letter of credit documentation) were excluded from this paper since they would not be appropriate as a comprehensive educational or training tool. For a listing of specialized programs excluded from our analysis, see Appendix B.

Once the programs were selected for analysis, the developers were then contacted and a demonstration copy and technical manual were requested for each program. All parties from whom a program was requested responded favorably, and there are no arrangements of any sort between the authors and any program developers.

The analysis of each program addresses the following key points:

- Program focus, objective and targeted user market
- Stage(s) of exporting process addressed
- Program features
- Strengths and weaknesses
- Application to case studies

To facilitate comparisons among programs, the exporting process was divided into five basic stages as follows:

1. *Internal assessment* by the prospective exporter, including competitive strengths and weaknesses on both an organizational and product basis (Kennen International 1991);
2. *International marketing research,* including the potential markets, competition, pricing, product planning, export and import trends, distribution and demographics;
3. *Market entry strategies* such as distribution, acquisition or joint venture strategies;
4. *Export strategy implementation,* including export documentation, licensing, insurance, financing, promotion and trade leads;
5. *Ongoing assessment of success or failure,* including performance measures and frequency of self-assessment process.

CASE STUDY APPLICATIONS

This paper develops several hypothetical case studies to highlight similarities and differences among programs and to serve as a guide to potential users by category (e.g., educators, advisors, businesses). These cases are described in further detail below.

Case One

The first case study involves a U.S. manufacturer of electronic components (spectrometers that measure energy emitted by certain sources) that does not presently export. The fictional company, Electronic Components Inc. ("ECI"), has $15 million in annual revenues and 50 employees. It wishes to learn more about the exporting process, to determine its readiness to export, to learn more about potential markets, and to understand the risks involved. This company has approached its local university which, as part of a graduate marketing class project, has assigned a team of students to assist the company. None of the students has any experience with exporting, and must also educate themselves before assisting the company.

Case Two

The second case study involves a manufacturer of biotechnology equipment that presently exports to several European countries.

This fictional company, Biotech Inc. ("BI"), wishes to search for additional markets in the Far East, Latin America, and elsewhere, but is uncertain about how to proceed. The company has contacted its local Department of Commerce office about resources to assist in the process, and has been informed that several software programs exist which can help it to assess these markets.

ANALYSIS OF PROGRAMS

The programs analyzed below are summarized in Table 1.

The National Trade Data Bank (NTDB)

The NTDB is a CD-ROM based service provided by the Department of Commerce which contains over 100,000 documents of current international trade and economic data from 15 federal government agencies. The program addresses all stages of the exporting process, with exceptional coverage of references and resources available to assist in the process. The stated objective of the NTDB is to provide reasonable public access, including electronic access, to federal government data of the greatest interest to U.S. firms that are engaged in export-related activities (Cremeans 1991 and Plant 1991). The NTDB's development was mandated by the enactment of legislation in 1988 that directed the Commerce Department to centralize the government's extensive trade and export promotion information resources housed in 15 separate agencies. The program is currently available at nearly 700 local libraries across the U.S. and is available free to any Federal Depository Library. The entire program is updated on a single disc each month and may be purchased as a monthly subscription or on a one-time basis. Its target market includes students and faculty of colleges and universities, businesses, and government agencies.

Program Features

The program is essentially a search and retrieval system for the extensive information maintained in the NTDB. It offers the user a choice of two search and retrieval features: "BROWSE," which is intended for users with basic computer skills and no specific knowl-

TABLE 1

Program Name	Developer/Marketer	Program Description	System Requirements
National Trade Data Bank	Office of Business Analysis U.S. Department of Commerce HCHB Room 4885 Washington, DC 20230 Contact: Mr. Ken Rogers Tel.: (202) 377-1986	CD-ROM based system which provides extensive economic and international trade data. Encompasses over 100,000 documents from 15 federal agencies; includes "how-to" guide for new exporters. Covers all stages of exporting process. Cost: $360/year or $35 for a single disc.	IBM PC's and compatibles. 640K available RAM. ISO 9660 CD-ROM reader (cost $500-800). MS-Software to access CD-ROM reader.
World Trade Exporter	National Technical Information Service and International Systems Development Corp. 2101 E. Jefferson St., Suite 210 Rockville, MD 20852 Contact: Mr. John Murdock Tel.: (301) 230-1373	Reference tool focusing on federal and state agency information that provides assistance to exporters. Link to over 850 external databases. Covers all stages of exporting process, with emphasis on research. Cost: $250 for basic system; $545 includes package of quarterly updates, WorldNet password, $100 on-line credit.	IBM PC's and compatibles. Operating system PC-DOS or MS-DOS version 3.0 or higher. 640K available RAM; hard disk with approx. 4.52 MB free space.

Name	Contact	Description	Requirements
World Trader	GateWaze Inc. 66 Summer Street, P.O. Box 743 Manchester, MA 01944 Contact: Mr. Charles Peers Tel. (800) 752-4711	Reference and planning tool covering all stages of the export process. Provides country profiles, trade data for the top 50 U.S. trading partners, key international trading contacts, an export reference guide, and hyper-menu linkages. Cost:$479 includes one year of quarterly updates and access to a toll-free hotline.	IBM PC's and compatibles. 640K available RAM. Hard disk storage space of 7 MB. EGA or VGA monitor.
Export to Win	Strategic Management Group, Inc. (with Port Authority of NY/NJ) 3624 Market Street Philadelphia, PA 19104 Contact: Ms. Kathryn Morgan Tel. (215) 387-4000	Computer-based simulation for students to learn about all stages of the exporting process. Encompasses five year period during which user builds export sales from nothing, confronting numerous obstacles. Cost: $99.95 retail price; $20 per student copy from South-Western Publishing (tel. 800-543-0487)	IBM PC's and compatibles. 640K available RAM. Hard or floppy disk drive.
CORE II	S. Tamer Cavusgil Michigan State University International Business Centers 6 Kellogg Center E. Lansing, MI 48824 Contact: Mr. Michel Mitri Tel.: (517) 353-4336	Assesses a company's readiness to export (corresponds to stage one of the exporting process). Self-assessment tool. Cost: $295	IBM PC's and compatibles. 580K available RAM. Hard disk with 2 MB disk space. 132 column printer.

edge of federal data; and "ROMWARE," a more complicated menu program that may be replaced in the near future. Both features search the NTDB database based on country, product, or topic criteria. This paper focuses on the BROWSE feature, a series of pyramid menu structures offering five different choices to access the database: *Source, Topic, Program, Subject* and *Item.* Selecting *Source* produces a detailed list of agencies contributing to the NTDB and serves as a gateway to a more detailed sub-menu of program names produced by each agency. *Topic* enables access by general topic or category, while *Subject* allows a search for more specific items (e.g., product or country).

The NTDB includes a comprehensive, 100 page guide to exporting as well as most resources published or maintained by the federal government on exporting. Included are such features as *The U.S. Industrial Outlook*; the *World Factbook* published by the Central Intelligence Agency detailing political, economic and cultural issues by country; market research reports on given countries and industries; and the *Foreign Traders Index,* which identifies over 50,000 foreign firms active or interested in importing U.S. products. The *Foreign Traders Index* also includes a description of each prospective importer by country and by product(s) desired, how long it has been in business, and the number of employees. The program is updated monthly.

Strengths

A key strength is the sheer volume of relevant, accessible trade and economic information housed in the program. As noted in the introduction of this paper, one of the critical gaps in export education to date has been organizing and distributing the volume of information maintained and assembled by the federal government. The NTDB addresses this problem in a surprisingly effective manner. The NTDB is especially appropriate for colleges and universities, many of which already have CD-ROM readers, for use in a broad number of curricula applications in economics, marketing and finance. In addition, as noted in the case study section below, both the electronic components and biotechnology equipment companies can fulfill their particular exporting information needs solely from this program.

Weaknesses

The NTDB program features only U.S. government information, and does not incorporate access to external databases or resources like World Trade Exporter or World Trader. A Department of Commerce spokesman notes that this exclusion is due to a desire to keep the costs of the NTDB reasonable, something it could not do by paying royalties to third party sources of information. The NTDB's search and retrieval software is also a bit more cumbersome than others. To be used effectively, the user must spend relatively more time reading the technical manual and working with the program, although the volume of information contained is also significantly greater and potentially more beneficial than in other programs. To use the database, one needs access to a CD-ROM reader, thereby excluding in the near-term many small and medium-sized businesses that have only basic personal computer setups. While these weaknesses may limit the program's effectiveness for business users, they do not diminish the appeal of this program for educational purposes. In addition, since the government applies no copyright protection to the information contained in the NTDB, it is expected (and encouraged by the Commerce Department) that a number of private software developers will begin to incorporate sections of the program relevant to small and medium-sized businesses into their current product offerings. The prices of CD-ROM readers are also expected to continue falling to more reasonable levels which, combined with more information becoming available on CD-ROM media, should encourage more businesses to purchase them.

Application to Case Studies

ECI would find enough information to sufficiently educate itself on the export process, although it would be advised to work through a regional U.S. Department of Commerce trade specialist to access this program. A first step of interest would be the twelve most common mistakes made by exporters, which is featured in the basic guide to exporting. For more specific information, the company could access the *Foreign Traders Index* to obtain a listing of spectrometer importers throughout the world. From the November

1991 NTDB disc, this company would be given a listing of eight importers specifically interested in spectrometers located in the Netherlands, Canada, Japan, the United Kingdom, Saudi Arabia, France, Chile and Belgium. No other program reviewed herein offers this level of detailed information. Market research could also be accessed by country. The program offers the ability to create mailing labels to companies on the *Foreign Traders Index* via WordPerfect version 5.1, a valuable feature.

The biotechnology company would similarly find a productive resource in the NTDB. In addition to detailed market research reports that could be accessed by product and country, it could access the *Foreign Traders Index* for a listing of biotechnology equipment importers. From the November 1991 NTDB disc, this company would be given a listing of twelve companies located in Denmark, Belgium, the Netherlands, Canada, Italy, India, the United Kingdom, and Japan. Again, no other program reviewed offered this detailed and productive level of information. Armed with the NTDB as a resource, the biotechnology equipment company could very quickly and efficiently conduct most steps of the market research process at a fraction of the cost in time and money of a third party consultant.

World Trade Exporter

World Trade Exporter is a comprehensive tool which provides references, resources and contacts dealing with all stages of the exporting process. The program's stated objective is "to assist small- and medium-sized U.S. businesses to become more competitive in the global business arena by providing the information critical to success in exporting." It is also recommended as an educational tool for universities and government agencies.

Program Features

World Trade Exporter has a superb menu-driven system which facilitates use and access of four main sections: Trade Topics, Trade Directory, Trade Bibliography, and NotePad. The *Trade Topics* section features 160 topics including a 44 page guide to the exporting process, a description of federal and state export assistance programs, a listing of products/services exported to major countries, and a calendar of trade fairs and shows. The *Trade Directory* is a name/address/telephone listing of 2,115 export-related agencies, organizations and contacts (public and private) in the U.S. and overseas that provide export information and assistance. The *Trade Bibliography* contains a listing of over 1,000 government and commercial on-line databases and 813 printed books and reports on international trade matters. The *NotePad* feature is a handy note-taking, recording and editing tool for personal notes and messages while working with the program.

The program also includes features to help the user to quickly locate, display and print out precise information through its powerful Search, Table of Contents, Glossary, Help and Keyboard Index features. These features can be accessed at any time from the main menu sections. Of particular interest, the *Trade Glossary* contains 372 exporting terms, functioning as a pop-up menu which can be accessed at any time as needed. The *Search* function is by far one of the most beneficial features of the program, enabling the user to quickly find the information being sought. World Trade Exporter also features a gateway to external communications through its modem function, which allows automatic log-on to the Worldnet ($545 package only) and Department of Commerce databases. The 151 page User's Guide is an excellent reference which includes a detailed 44 page tutorial on using the system.

Strengths

The program is one of the more comprehensive yet easy to use of the systems reviewed. Its menu, search, glossary and communications features are powerful yet easy to use, enabling the user to quickly and efficiently find the information or resources sought. The program does not seek to contain all primary information available to current or prospective exporters, but rather acts as a comprehensive research and reference vehicle. The volume of information stored in the program is also impressive. The pop-up features were well thought out, especially the Glossary section which can be accessed when needed. The system is also updated quarterly, a service included in the $545 purchase price.

Weaknesses

No glaring weaknesses were found with this program. One mild bias is to point the prospective or current exporter mainly toward governmental resources, which the developer notes is a program objective. Given the high quality and low price of such resources this is not a weakness, however. The program could be strengthened by incorporating certain contacts and topics covered in more depth by the NTDB, especially the *Foreign Traders Index*. By combining World Trade Exporter's search capability with the raw data contained in the NTDB, an even more outstanding program for educational, business and government users could be created. We understand that the developer is presently working to incorporate access to the NTDB into the program.

World Trade Exporter does not profess to go into the depth that some other systems do to exhaustively describe the exporting process, although it does devote 44 pages to an effective overview and provides extensive resources and references for additional information. ISDC also publishes the *World Trade Director* program which is similar to World Trade Exporter except that it addresses more of the process of exporting and less of the references and resources contained in World Trade Exporter. Given this similarity, *World Trade Director* was not reviewed in this paper.

Application to Case Studies

This program is highly relevant and beneficial to both case study examples. In the case of ECI, a review of the basics contained in the "Learning Exporting" section would offer a good overview of the process and suggest an appropriate first step: using an export qualifier program (CORE II). To obtain a contact for CORE II, we used the search function in the Directory, where we found a telephone number for the U.S. & Foreign Commercial Services in Washington, D.C. Calling this number, we were immediately referred to the Philadelphia district U.S. Commerce Department office, which administers the CORE II program in our region. The program also would direct ECI to a number of resources from which it could learn more about international market research, market entry strategies, financing, trade leads and general success tips.

In addition to this general information, a more specific search of the Trade Topics and Bibliography sections under the general category "Components" would direct the user to a number of resources including several state International Trade Administration offices and to countries which import components (Algeria, Australia, Austria, Canada, France, Israel, Singapore, Taiwan and Thailand). The Trade Calendar section of the Trade Topics menu would direct the user to six international trade shows featuring electronic components, including one in March 1992 in Seoul, Korea and one in April 1992 in Utrecht, Netherlands. In addition to these leads, a search of the Bibliography section would produce 13 publications regarding foreign markets for components, such as export opportunities in Europe. These are excellent leads and exemplify the utility of this program, which also provides easy-to-use print capabilities to record these leads on paper. It should be noted that the *World Trader* program reviewed on the following page yields greater potential contacts in this specific case study than World Trade Exporter: a similar search of countries importing electronic components produced 21 countries and 13 trade shows versus 9 and 2, respectively, for World Trade Exporter. The reader should also keep in mind that the NTDB system is by far the most complete resource for investigating potential export markets, producing more potential and specific leads than either World Trader or World Trade Exporter.

For the biotechnology equipment company, World Trade Exporter would also be a valuable source of data. Singapore and the United Kingdom are biotechnology equipment export markets mentioned in the Trade Topics section, while in the Bibliography section 18 publications regarding foreign markets would be identified. In addition, this company would be referred to the U.S. & Foreign Commercial Services' Comparison Shopping Service, which provides the detailed information needed to assess export markets in over 50 countries.

World Trader

World Trader is a comprehensive reference tool which assists its users in understanding the exporting process, identifying export markets, explaining important trade issues, and obtaining trade contacts in foreign countries. The program appeals to small, medium

and large businesses; lawyers, consultants, accountants and government agents who advise these businesses; and educators and students in business programs.

Program Features

World Trader is composed of four primary program segments:
World Atlas, Market Analyst, Info-Deck, and *Export Reference
Guide,* data in which are integrated by *Quick-Link,* a powerful
data-linking tool. *World Atlas* contains general information profiles
on over 125 countries, including country overviews, import statistics,
transportation and communication access, and regional maps. *Market Analyst* offers the ability to analyze trade data by country on such
search criteria as prospects by product category, total imports, and
total U.S. imports. This is useful for determining on a macro sense
where the export markets are for various U.S. products. A charting
feature facilitates organizing and presenting data for selected countries, while data can also be downloaded to ASCII, Lotus 1-2-3 or
dBase files. *Info-Deck* is organized as an electronic file directory of
over 3,500 U.S. and foreign trade contacts which can be printed from
the Global Report Generator feature. The *Export Reference Guide,* a
677 page reference source on all stages of the exporting process, is
included in the software. The guide is based on the publication
Exportise by the Small Business Foundation of America, a 272 page
written copy of which is included in the User's Guide to World
Trader. To provide an overview of the *Export Reference Guide,* the
program offers an unique *Blueprint* feature which is a high level
schematic of the exporting process linked to sections of the guide. It
provides an excellent overview; the user can also access any stage of
the exporting process shown in the schematic simply by moving the
cursor and pressing return. *Quick-Link* enables the user to link data
among the four program segments.

The program also features helpful pop-up utilities which include
calculators for distance between any two cities in the world, weights
and measures and foreign currency conversions, and time zone for
any city; an easily accessible glossary of trade terms; and a search
mode to access a detailed database of over 2,500 international trade
show listings.

Strengths

World Trader is a well designed reference tool packed with valuable features. Like World Trade Exporter, it is easier to learn and use to access trade information than the NTDB system, although this may be due in part to the fact that it houses about one-tenth the information of the NTDB. *World Atlas* is an excellent feature which can quickly educate the user on general matters about foreign countries, although it contains considerably less detail in this area than either the NTDB or *Passport* (described in Appendix B) systems. *Info-Deck* has excellent trade contacts arranged in a branching hierarchy for easy access, including for example a detailed listing of freight forwarders.

Weaknesses

Although the program does not contain any glaring weaknesses, several areas for improvement are suggested. First, the user searching for export markets can quickly generate a listing of all countries that import a general product category. It is not possible to view on screen a summary of the search findings for more than five countries at a time, however. Instead, the results must be output to a data file or to a printer. Data for a single country can be displayed, or up to five countries' import data can be compared on screen using the *Chart* feature. Second, the program offers good general information on countries importing a general product category (e.g., Electronics and Electronic Components), but offers neither the specificity of product (e.g., spectrometer) nor the vast importer contacts contained in the NTDB system. World Trade Exporter also shares this weakness. Both World Trader and World Trade Exporter would benefit from providing greater access to the NTDB system within their programs.

Application to Case Studies

The electronic components company and its student assistants would benefit significantly from World Trader. The trade references and exporting guide are outstanding and thorough. Regarding market research, World Trader would offer a listing of 21 countries that import electronics and electronic components. This list would be an excellent resource from which to conduct additional research. Interestingly, the list of 21 countries found by the program is much broader than the 9 countries generated by the World Trade Exporter program, and the number of trade shows found is 13 compared with six for World Trade Exporter. World Trade Exporter's bibliography feature provides more external references to assist both case study companies, however. In summary, both the company and the students would find this program to be of great assistance.

The biotechnology company would also find the program of assistance in its effort to expand international markets, and similar to World Trade Exporter would find two countries (United Kingdom and Singapore) that represent potential new markets. The references in this program would generally point our company in the correct direction, although the NTDB system offered more specific and detailed information, including importer contacts, as noted above.

Export To Win! (Student Edition)

Export To Win!/Student Edition is a complete system that addresses all stages of the exporting process. It is the only software simulation among the programs evaluated. The program's stated objectives for its users are threefold: (1) to learn that exporting makes good business sense; (2) to learn about the importance of research and developing an international marketing plan; and (3) to discover how proper export management will permit global marketing. The program targets educators in college and university business programs. There is little difference, however, between the student edition and the professional edition, the target markets of which are businesses, government agencies, and export advisory firms.

Program Features

The simulation assumes no prior knowledge of exporting and very little proficiency in using a computer. The user acts as the marketing manager of Xebec Company, a U.S. manufacturer of industrial process control equipment with $13.5 million in annual sales. Xebec, which has never exported, faces declining growth opportunities in the U.S. Xebec's Chairman has directed the marketing manager to head up the company's exporting effort and to reach $6 million in export sales within five years, the period covered by the simulation. The marketing manager must put together a marketing plan and make a number of critical decisions over the five year period (which actually takes 4-6 hours to finish), the results of which are measured in annual income statements. The simulation is complemented by a 63 page written manual which includes a glossary of key exporting terms, over 100 relevant external references and resources, quiz and study questions, and an instructor's manual. The menus are well constructed, enabling the user to delve deeper into marketing theory concepts from the simulation.

The program covers many relevant marketing topics and concepts. Year One of the simulation covers the advantages of exporting, Xebec's competitive position, and a decision on whether to visit a domestic or foreign trade show. In Year Two, the user receives a request for an export quote from a French company and starts the process of pricing, investigating export licensing, determining whether to sell on open account or via a letter of credit, deciding how to sell and ship the product, and selecting insurance coverage. In Year Three, market research is evaluated, a distribution network is established, an export manager is hired, and export management companies are reviewed. Year Four covers foreign travel and culture, currency exchange, market planning and promotion. Year Five involves product development, tracking industry trends, and strategic planning.

Strengths

The program meets its three stated objectives in a satisfactory manner. It has a high degree of proficiency in teaching the user about the process of exporting. It has a fairly good index to additional resources and references on the exporting process, although not nearly as comprehensive and accessible as the NTDB, World Trader and World Trade Exporter. The simulated, real-world experiences contained in Export To Win! offer the user a unique learning environment not found in other programs. For further research covering the use of simulation in teaching business principles, see Haslam (1990), Burgess (1991) and Faria (1987). Export To Win! also reinforces a number of critical marketing concepts taught on both the undergraduate and graduate levels.

Weaknesses

In general, the program when compared to others is less comprehensive and sophisticated. The pricing simulation is the weakest aspect of the program. While the simulation offers an excellent lesson on pricing theory, and provides several alternatives for allocating overhead costs, there is no realism in the actual price that the user can set for Xebec's product. The program shows that Xebec's competitors all sell their product for $5,800, and that Xebec's cost-plus pricing would range from a low of $5,552 to a high of $5,930. Yet the user can input any price up to $999,999 and the foreign buyer will always come back and accept two units for $500 less than quoted. As a result, students do not gain an appreciation of real-world pricing.

The program rarely allows the user to make any serious mistakes: if the user selects the "wrong" decision (e.g., declining to learn more about competitors) the program immediately offers a prompt suggesting that the user may want to change the decision. While this facilitates the simulation, it might be more beneficial if the user learned the hard way. A related weakness is that once a year's simulation has been completed and the user has progressed to the next year, it is impossible to go back to any previous years to make modifications. While this makes the simulation more realistic, it also makes it more difficult to do "what if" scenarios by changing certain variables.

The program gives inadequate focus to promotion, assuming that these efforts will be handled mostly by the foreign distributor. It gives no suggestions on how to evaluate foreign distributors, although some of the references cited deal with this issue. Marketing research is not stressed until the third year, long after Xebec has made its first export sales. While this is not necessarily atypical of how the real world operates, the simulation would serve its users better by emphasizing the importance of internal assessment and research at the beginning of the process, and by referring users to resources such as the CORE II program. Notwithstanding these weaknesses, the program as priced represents a good value and a useful teaching tool.

Application to Case Studies

ECI's student assistants would benefit from using Export To Win! as a first step in the exporting process. The program provides a satisfactory overview of many of the issues that will be faced by the prospective exporter. Its positive, upbeat orientation would potentially motivate the students and the components company to investigate exporting in greater detail. The resources and references provided in the written manual offer sufficient contacts to address many of the concerns of this company and in fact to position it for successful exporting. Given its attractive price relative to the information provided, the program is an especially valuable self-study aid that could be used with minimal supervision to familiarize students, especially on the undergraduate level, with the basics of the exporting process. It does not contain the comprehensive contacts, references and resources of the NTDB, World Trader, and World Trade Exporter programs that may be appropriate for graduate-level students, however.

The program would be moderately beneficial to the biotechnology equipment company in the second case study due to the references and resources that could direct this firm to the information it needs. However, since it already exports we believe that the NTDB, World Trader, and World Trade Exporter programs may be more appropriate resources.

CORE II (Company Readiness to Export)

CORE II addresses internal assessment and positioning, the first stage of the exporting process. It is designed to be used as a management tool for assessing a company's readiness to export. The program's stated objective is to assist both potential exporters and advisors to exporters in developing a systematic, proactive approach to export market development. CORE II targets the following user groups: (a) individual companies interested in evaluating their own readiness to export; (b) export assistance agencies interested in helping their clients evaluate and prepare for exporting; and (c) colleges, universities and seminar/workshop sponsors seeking an educational tool to explore the exporting process.

Program Features

The program starts by offering the user the choice of "novice" or "expert" mode, the difference being that novice mode offers additional instructions throughout the exercise. For an export assistance agency or consulting firm that regularly uses the program, this is a beneficial, time-saving feature. The user then starts from a Main Menu, the centerpiece of the program, which offers two principal choices: commencing the CORE II exercise (the evaluation of export readiness) or a step-by-step export guide. If the user is unfamiliar with even the basic concepts of exporting, the step-by-step tutorial guide serves as a good overview in outline form of all stages of the exporting process. It is by no means a comprehensive resource, however.

The CORE II exercise emphasizes up front that five factors are highly correlated with exporting success: (a) the organizational characteristics of the firm; (b) the motivation for going international; (c) top management commitment; (d) the company's product strengths; and (e) the suitability of its products for foreign customers. The user then provides responses to a detailed five section survey which corresponds to the five success factors. The program reminds the user to give candid responses in order to provide an objective assessment of the company's export potential. Once a section of the survey has been completed, a message appears on the screen summarizing what has just been covered and how it relates to exporting success. In addition, CORE II offers the ability to review and modify user responses at any time. After answering the first section dealing with background questions, the program points out three factors that are generally associated with exporting success: (a) risk taking attitudes of managers; (b) the firm's expansion in the domestic market; and (c) access to experienced personnel and resources. It also reminds the user that one must have a deliberate strategy to achieve specific goals in exporting. The user is then prompted to enter the principal product category of the firm, and is offered six choices: "Components, Commercial Products (e.g., office equipment, computers, furniture), Industrial Goods, Agricultural Goods, Final Consumer Products, and Services." Our hypothetical producers of spectrometers and biotechnology equipment might be confused about which category they fall under, and no assistance is offered by the generic help feature.

Once the five-part survey has been completed, the user proceeds to the *CORE II Evaluation,* which weights the responses given and generates both a graphical matrix and a more detailed written breakdown of the company's export readiness rating (high, moderate or low) in two categories: Organizational and Product. These categories measure success factors such as previous international experience, strength of motivation for exporting, management commitment, product uniqueness and product adaptability. The more detailed written breakdown offers readiness ratings and composite scores for the five success factors. Once the evaluation section has been started, the user is not allowed to return to the main menu until it has been completed.

Strengths

Depending on the accuracy of the answers to the survey, the program can provide a good assessment of how ready a company is to export before it haphazardly enters into the process. It identifies potential company weaknesses, which top management can address prior to entering international markets. It points out certain of the company's strengths which can be exploited in export markets. CORE II allows the user to choose different responses to the survey (e.g., higher or lower level of management commitment) and observe the changes in the degree of export readiness. It also provides a basic tutorial on all steps of the exporting process. For export agencies and consulting firms, the program offers the ability to provide a written input form to interested companies, a valuable feature that can save time as well as appeal to those with no desire or ability to use a computer. The help feature offers educational explanations of many topics, and is only infrequently too general to offer specific assistance. A written user manual is provided which has a helpful introduction and guide to using the program.

Weaknesses

The CORE II program is an effective tool for assessing the factors correlated with exporting success, and for identifying strengths and weaknesses of the prospective exporter. It is unlikely to be as valuable a learning tool for students of international business, however, unless a detailed case study can be prepared which provides input for the survey points. The detailed nature of the questions on the company, management's motivation and commitment, and product strengths do not lend themselves to reactive impulse answers, and little educational benefit is derived. The program offers only limited references to external information. In addition, the step-by-step tutorial is more of an outline and not of sufficient depth to provide a comprehensive education in the exporting process for students.

The written manual also notes that the program asks for limited information from the user company and that it provides only a tentative positioning of the company's organizational and product strengths and weaknesses. Accordingly, it advises that the program should be used with an experienced export advisor so that positive or negative results are not to be misinterpreted as conclusive. The risk, however, is that a prospective exporter without an experienced advisor might be dissuaded from further evaluation if a low readiness rating was received.

Application to Case Studies

CORE II is highly recommended for ECI and would be educational for the team of students involved in assisting the company. By design, the program is intended to address only the first stage of the exporting process, and ECI and the students must look to another program for assistance in other stages of the exporting process. Similarly, the step-by-step export guide discusses the overall process only in very general terms, and does not provide a detailed listing of external references and resources. In the second case, BI already exports and presumably meets the readiness tests.

Therefore, CORE II would not have much apparent value to this firm. The program's developer, Dr. Cavusgil, commented however that it might be beneficial to have the managers of this company complete the CORE II assessment to compare their perceptions of success factors with the CORE II results and to see if these coincide. In addition, Dr. Cavusgil noted that CORE II can be used as an assessment tool to delineate how individual managers perceive their company's strengths and weaknesses, with the results of each individual compared and contrasted with others.

CONCLUSION AND RECOMMENDATIONS

Table 2 provides a summary which rates the relative proficiency of each program along two lines: (a) general features and benefits and (b) effectiveness in assisting the hypothetical case study companies. All the programs reviewed were generally found to be well designed and successful in meeting their program objectives. As noted in the introduction, this paper is intended to meet the needs of educators and students in undergraduate and graduate business programs. It is also applicable to businesses looking to enter or expand into export markets and to government agencies and other advisors involved in export education and administration. Which programs are most appropriate for each of these groups?

Business school educators would be well served by investigating the NTDB system in greater detail. Many universities throughout the U.S. maintain CD-ROM readers in library reference areas, and the NTDB system could be used more broadly in economics, marketing and international business curricula. World Trade Exporter should be investigated in part for its powerful search feature and extensive bibliography, as well as its ease of use. World Trader, similar to World Trade Exporter in certain respects, also merits evaluation. Export To Win! represents an excellent value ($20 per student copy) and could be used as a course supplement in a foundations course to save class time by enabling students to cover the exporting process on their own.

Businesses would be advised to investigate (in the following order) World Trade Exporter, World Trader, the NTDB and Export

TABLE 2

PROFICIENCY RATINGS (1=OUTSTANDING, 2=SATISFACTORY, 3=BELOW AVERAGE) *

	The NTDB	World Trade Exporter	World Trader	Export To Win	CORE II**
1. General Features/Benefits					
Stages of export process addressed:					
o Internal assessment	2	2	2.5	3	1
o Market research	1	1.5	1.5	2.5	
o Entry strategies	2	2	2	2	
o Strategy implementation	2	2	2	2	
o Ongoing assessment	2	2	2	2	
User's guide/technical manual	3	2	1	2	2
Menu/help features	2	1	1	2	2
Data search feature	2	1	2	3	
Content: depth and breadth	1	2	2	2.5	1
Ease of navigating program	2	1	1	1	1
Teaching effectiveness	1	1	1	1.5	1

2. Case 1 Items

Learn about exporting process	1	2	2	1.5	2
Determine export readiness	2	2	2.5	3	1
Learn about potential markets	1	2	2	2.5	
Understand risks involved	2	2	2	1.5	2

3. Case 2 Items

Search for new export markets	1	2	2	2.5	

* Proficiency ratings by the authors of this paper.

** This program does not attempt to address all stages of the exporting process and is evaluated only for criteria which apply.

To Win! They should also keep in mind that CORE II is a recommended first step appropriate for every company considering exporting, and that the Passport system, although not reviewed herein due to its specialization, is a valuable aid in understanding foreign cultures and business practices (see Appendix B for a brief description).

Businesses should also seek to utilize the resources of the government provided through the Department of Commerce. As a general rule, a company seeking export information or assistance should first seek to take advantage of the vast resources, many of them free of charge, that are offered by the federal government. Many of these services are provided on a regional basis, supplemented by small business export development centers maintained in a number of universities around the U.S. These resources are well equipped to offer appropriate education and assistance, and frequently offer access to or use of many of the programs reviewed herein at a fraction of the charge of purchasing them outright.

Government agencies would be wise to invest the resources to promote more widespread usage of the NTDB and Export Qualifier (CORE II) programs by private sector software developers. In addition, government agencies should be aware of the private sector programs available so that they may be recommended where appropriate.

REFERENCES

Burgess, T.E. (1991). The Use of Computerized Management and Business Simulation in the United Kingdom. *Simulation and Games, 22* (2), 174-195.

Cavusgil, S.T. (1987). Qualitative Insights into Company Experiences in International Marketing Research. *Journal of Business & Industrial Marketing, 2* (Summer), 41-54.

Cremeans, J. & Williams, A. (1991). The National Trade Data Bank: A New Window on International Trade. *CD-Rom Professional* (July), 76-80.

Dekkers, J. & Donnatti, S. (1981). The Integration of Research Studies on the Use of Simulation as an Instructional Strategy. *Journal of Education Research, 74*, 424-427.

Faria, A.J. (1987). A Survey of the Use of Business Games in Academia and Business. *Simulation and Games, 18* (2), 207-224.

Haslam, E.L. (1990). The Case For Simulation. *CBT Directions* (September) 10-16.

Holstein, W. & Kelly, K. (1992, April 13). Little Companies, Big Exporters. *Business Week*, pp. 70-72.

International Council for Computers in Education (Ed.). (1986). *Software Selection, Evaluation and Organization (and) Software Reviews. Article Reprints.* Eugene, OR: International Council for Computers in Education.

Karakaya, F. & Karakaya, F. (1989). Selection of Statistical Software Package for Marketing Research Course. In Dwyer, F.R. & Steinberg, M., *Proceedings of the 1989 AMA Microcomputers in the Marketing Curriculum Conference* (pp. 237-244). Chicago, IL: American Marketing Association.

Kefalas, A.G. & Carr, H.H. (1988). Designing an Assistant Export Expert Information System (EXIS) for an International Manager. In Sprague, R., *Proceedings of the Twenty-First Annual Hawaii International Conference on System Sciences IEEE* (pp. 94-101). Washington, DC: IEEE Comput. Soc. Press.

Kennen International, Cavusgil, S.T., & The Dialog Systems Division of A.T. Kearny, Inc. (1991). CORE II USER'S GUIDE, Version 3.2.

Li, T. & Cavusgil, S.T. (1991). International Marketing: A Classification of Research Streams and Assessment of Development Since 1982. In Gilley, C.F., Dwyer, F.R., Leigh, T.W., Dubinsky, A.J., Richins, M.L., Curry, D. & Venkatesh, A. *1991 AMA Educators' Proceedings: Enhancing Knowledge Development in Marketing* (pp. 164-175). Chicago, IL: American Marketing Association.

Mitri, M., Evirgen, T.C., Cavusgil, S.T. (1991). The Country Consultant: An Expert System for the International Marketing Executive. In *1991 AMA Educators' Proceedings: Enhancing Knowledge Development in Marketing* (pp. 21-33). Chicago, IL: American Marketing Association.

Mitri, M., Yeoh, P., Oszomer, A. & Cavusgil, S.T. (1991). Expert Systems in International Marketing. In *1991 AMA Educators' Proceedings: Enhancing Knowledge Development in Marketing* (pp. 164-175). Chicago, IL: American Marketing Association.

Plant, M. (1991). The National Trade Data Bank: A One Year Perspective. *Business America* (September), 2-5.

Redmond, W.H. (1989). On the duration of Simulations: An Exploration of Minimum Effective Length. *Journal of Marketing Education, 11* (Spring) 53-57.

Reiman, V. (1991, June 10). SMG turns computer simulations into real profits. *The Philadelphia Inquirer,* pp. 1-c, 7-c.

The Exporter Magazine (Producer) (1989). *The Exporters Guide to Computer Software and Services for the Export Business.* New York, NY.

Weber, J. (1991). Global Business Simulation (GBSIM): A Simulation Exercise to Aid in Globalizing the Marketing Curriculum. In Dwyer, F.R. & Steinberg, M., *Proceedings of the 1989 AMA Microcomputers in the Marketing Curriculum Conference* (pp. 59-71). Chicago, IL: American Marketing Association.

APPENDIX A

DESCRIPTION OF SOURCES

Sources of information included the U.S. Department of Commerce, software developers, publishers, educators and private sector consultants. As a result of interviews with and contacts suggested by these sources, we developed a listing of individuals who would know most about the existence of comprehensive international trade software programs. We were forced to rely on these sources due to the limited published information on the newly developed programs. When no new contacts or sources were suggested, the interviews were stopped. From these experts, a listing of software programs was developed which was then screened against our selection criteria.

We would like to acknowledge the assistance of the following sources: Mr. Hans H.B. Koehler, Wharton Export Network; Mr. Robert Kistler and Mr. Rodney Stuart, International Trade Administration; Mr. L. Stroh, publisher, *The Exporter Magazine*; Ms. Homa Tavangar, Chester County (PA) International Initiative; Mr. Bruce Cooper, *Computers in Education*; Mr. David Rogers, Ph.D., *Computers and Education*; Mr. S. Tamer Cavusgil, Ph.D., and Mr. Michel Mitri, Michigan State University International Business Centers; Mr. Michael Morin, Kennen International; Ms. Terri Morrison, Getting Through Customs; Mr. Ken Harris, MK Technologies Inc.; Mr. Philip Ferzan and Ms. Joanna Kamarimopoulos, NJ Division of International Trade; Mr. Ken Rogers, Office of Business Analysis, U.S. Department of Commerce; Ms. Kathryn Morgan, Strategic Management Group Inc.; Ms. Mary Smolenski, Computer Industry Analyst, U.S. Department of Commerce; Ms. Blair Nair, World Trade Institute; Mr. Richard Horan, Xport (Port Authority of NY/NJ); Ms. Laurie Caswell and Mr. John Murdock, International Systems Development Corp.; Ms. Katie Van Auken and Mr. Charles Peers, GateWaze Inc.; Ms. Barbara Moebious, Associate Dean, International Trade, Waukesha County Technical College; Mr. Mike Uretsky, Ph.D., New York University and principal, Business Simulations, Inc.

APPENDIX B

SPECIALIZED PROGRAMS EXCLUDED FROM ANALYSIS

The Exporter Magazine (1989) lists over one hundred software programs under the categories of export management, trade finance, sales support, distribution management and communications. The Finders program, freely distributed by the U.S. Department of Agriculture (Economic Research Services), focuses on agricultural matters. The Global Data Manager program (World Game Institute, Philadelphia, PA), the largest commercially available compilation of global statistics for use on a personal computer, focuses on statistics and not on the exporting process. Weber (1991) describes the Global Business Simulation (GBSIM) program, which has players predict changes in the value of the dollar against other major world currencies and to make fictitious trades in the actual currency futures or options markets. The Passport system provides cultural, political, business practice, travel and medical information on over fifty countries to foreign business travelers (contact Getting Through Customs, telephone 215-353-9894).

In addition, we are aware of several developmental programs which due to space constraints are not reviewed in this paper. The Michigan State University International Business Centers has been developing several expert systems (Mitri, Yeoh, Oszomer & Cavusgil (1991) and Mitri, Evirgen & Cavusgil (1991)). Kefalas (1988) discusses another expert system, The Export Information System.

Electronic Data Retrieval in International Business Education: Prospects and Resources

Fred Miller

Linda Gillespie Miller

SUMMARY. Successful international business executives thrive on timely information. It is very important, therefore, that international business students be able to gather global company and market information and apply it to decision making in class assignments. Though electronic data retrieval is the most efficient and effective way to gather data on this scale, it is an underutilized microcomputer application. This study evaluates the two most important means of electronic data retrieval, CD ROM and online data retrieval. It also identifies some databases available through these means and describes how they may be used in assignments in international business classes.

INTRODUCTION

Online and CD ROM data retrieval techniques have not yet realized their full potential within the business curriculum. They have a

---

Fred Miller is affiliated with the Department of Management and Marketing at Murray State University, Murray, KY 42071. Linda Gillespie Miller is a Doctoral Candidate at the University of Kentucky, and Systems Analyst, University Development and Administrative Services, Murray State University.

[Haworth co-indexing entry note]: "Electronic Data Retrieval in International Business Education: Prospects and Resources." Miller, Fred, and Linda Gillespie Miller. Co-published simultaneously in the *Journal of Teaching in International Business* (The Haworth Press, Inc.) Vol. 4, No. 3/4, 1993, pp. 85-101; and: *Utilizing New Information Technology in Teaching of International Business: A Guide for Instructors* (ed: Fahri Karakaya and Erdener Kaynak) The Haworth Press, Inc., 1993, pp. 85-101. Multiple copies of this article/chapter may be purchased from The Haworth Document Delivery Center. Call 1-800-3-HAWORTH (1-800-342-9678) between 9:00 - 5:00 (EST) and ask for DOCUMENT DELIVERY CENTER.

85

particular strong contribution to make in international business courses in that they provide timely, comprehensive access to information on world markets. This study: (1) discusses the value of these techniques; (2) assesses the merits of CD ROM and online methods of data retrieval; and (3) identifies important resources for class-related research in international business.

ELECTRONIC DATA RETRIEVAL
IN INTERNATIONAL BUSINESS EDUCATION

Within the area of microcomputer applications in business education, the application with the greatest discrepancy between potential and practice is electronic data retrieval. This is particularly true in the field of international business, where information is the life's blood of successful strategic and tactical planning (Drucker, 1985). In all its forms, electronic data retrieval provides timely access to large bodies of information more efficiently than physical searches in corresponding printed references. For international business research, the advantages are even more pronounced, as print versions of the relevant databases do not exist, the journals indexed are hard to find, and original articles may be published in several different languages, (Daniels, 1984; Large, 1990; O'Leary, 1986; Spickard, 1987). These techniques may also serve as the most cost effective technologies of information transfer to support research activities in developing countries (Barcellos, 1989; Nicholls and Majid, 1989).

Despite this potential, these tools have not been widely integrated into the business curriculum. Teaching of microcomputer applications has concentrated on data analysis tools at the expense of data collection tools (Miller, 1985; Doney and Ross, 1987; Kurtz and Boone, 1987; Salton, 1987). Though the importance of electronic data retrieval in gathering competitive intelligence has been recognized (Miller, 1987) and several "how-to" studies have appeared (Edyburn, 1988; Johnson, 1989; Miller, 1989; Oley, 1989), this application has not become widely used in business education (Dyer, 1987; Kurtz and Boone, 1987).

While no study has probed for the reasons why this specific microcomputer technology is underutilized, the general reasons found by

Kurtz and Boone (1987) are probably at work here. Those factors are: (1) lack of faculty familiarity: (2) lack of faculty time; and (3) costs. In each of these areas, however, developments of recent years have lowered these barriers considerably. The following section discusses advances which have decreased the learning time and cost associated with electronic data retrieval. After that, a description of the resources available for electronic research in international business will provide information to faculty in this field.

THE STATUS OF ELECTRONIC
DATA RETRIEVAL TECHNOLOGIES

The two basic forms of electronic data retrieval are CD ROM and online database searching. In the first, data is retrieved from compact disc databases which are read by appropriate drives attached to personal computers. In the second, a local computer accesses data stored in larger systems in off-site locations. The relative merits of each approach are assessed by Miller (May, 1989). They may be summarized as follows.

The equipment for a CD ROM system can be relatively expensive, though costs have fallen in recent years and continue on a downward track. Costs for drives with requisite hardware and software lie in the $400 to $700 range. Costs for general reference CD's have fallen drastically, with many having prices of under $100. Bundling pricing policies by drive manufacturers and/or retailers can produce costs that are even lower than this. More specialized research databases have significantly higher prices, though these too are falling. The number of research databases being published in CD ROM form is also increasing (Wiley, 1989), as is number of available CD ROM search facilities in the United States and western Europe (Chen and Raitt, 1990). Moreover, many government documents are now published as CD's. Perhaps the most significant example for international business is the United States Department of Commerce's "National Trade Data Bank," a collection of 100,000 different documents. Its cost is $35 per single disk, or $360 for 12 monthly upgrades each year (Plant, 1991).

Though these costs are relatively high, they are also fixed. Variable costs are limited to supplies such as diskettes and paper. This technology allows students to learn search techniques without incurring high online charges. Personal computer operating systems allow data from CD ROM sources to be merged with other PC applications quickly and easily. Graphics are much more widely accessible on CD ROM than online databases, while cross referencing and hypertext applications are also more common. On the down side, the only way to update a CD ROM database is to replace it. The number of databases available is limited by the available budget, and the use of each CD is limited to one person at a time.

The cost structure for online data retrieval is the exact opposite of that for CD ROM. For current microcomputer users, equipment costs are limited to a modem and the software to run it. At present, $200 amply meets this need and includes 9600 baud send/receive fax capability as well. Several international trade data resources, such as the Trade Data Exchange and the World Trade Centers' interactive trade leads system, are available at little cost. More significant for classroom purposes, however, are the DIALOG Business Connection (DBC) and Classroom Instruction Program (CIP) offered by DIALOG Information Services. Described at some length by Miller (May, 1989), these programs offer access to most of DIALOG's 200+ databases at a fixed fee of $15 per connect hour. The DIALOG Business Connection, in particular, is remarkably easy to use and provides access to a wide range of information on international companies and markets to novice searchers. The next section describes some of the databases included in these programs.

Online data retrieval has several advantages over CD ROM. Users have access to several hundred databases without incurring the incremental charge of purchasing each one. These databases are constantly updated at no additional charge to the user. Several related databases may be searched simultaneously, and, in the case of the DBC, transparently. Finally, through separate systems, several users can access the same databases simultaneously.

On the other hand, online data retrieval does have some problems. Outside the DBC, faculty and students must learn to use searching techniques efficiently to develop search strategies. Further, even at the $15 per hour rate, some concern must be given to password security to avoid unlimited, costly searches by students. With only a few exceptions (Thompson, 1989), most online databases are text based, with few graphics applications. Finally, management and printing of search files is more difficult in an online system than a CD ROM one.

This discussion should not imply that these technologies are mutually exclusive alternatives. At present prices and with the current downward trend, they may well be complementary tools in training students to gather data electronically. Search techniques developed on selected CD ROM products will make students more accomplished online searchers. International business instructors could easily use low cost CD ROM general reference and government sources in conjunction with more extensive market related research in online databases. Indeed, as 56.8% of academic libraries in the United States have CD ROM capability (Chen and Raitt, 1990), many students may already be familiar with this technology. Their skills could be expanded to international business research through the purchase of the low cost general reference and government CD ROM products mentioned above.

USING DIALOG DATABASES IN INTERNATIONAL BUSINESS EDUCATION

This section describes ways in which databases from the DIALOG information system may be used in international business courses and assignments. While not comprehensive, Figure 1 lists the DIALOG databases which are most relevant for research in international business courses. The DIALOG database system is chosen for its wide and growing collection of databases related to international business, its low cost and virtually universal accessibility. Further, many of the databases in Figure 1 are included in the DIALOG Business Connection system, rendering them easily available to inexperienced searchers.

There are four general types of international business research in which electronic data retrieval can be useful. They are: (1) market assessment; (2) financial analysis of companies; (3) identifying potential opportunities, support services, customers, partners and/or competitors; and (4) competitive analysis. In the market assessment research, students evaluate foreign countries as markets in general

FIGURE 1: SELECTED DIALOG DATABASES WITH INTERNATIONAL BUSINESS INFORMATION

Database (DIALOG Number)	Geographic Focus	Type of Information
ABI Inform (15)	International	Academic literature in business
AGRIS International (203)	International	Agricultural literature
Arab Information Bank (465)	Arab world	Economic, political, social trends
Asia Pacific (30)	Asia/Pacific rim	Business and economic news
Business International (627)	International	Economic, political, social, & business trends
Canadian Business and Current Affairs (262)	Canada	Business and general news
CANCORP Canadian Corporations (491)	Canada	Corporate directory
Corporate Affiliations (513)	International	Corporate parent/subsidiary relationships
D&B Canadian Dun's Market Identifiers (520)	Canada	Corporate directory, some financial information
D&B European Dun's Market Identifiers (521)	Europe	Corporate directory
D&B International Dun's Market Identifiers (518)	International	Corporate directory
Delphes European Business (481)	Europe	Business and economic news (French language)
DIALOG Company Name Finder (416)	International	Identifies databases with information on a selected company

Title	Region	Description
European Directory of Agrochemicals (316)	Europe	Directory of agrochemical products
Extel International Financial Cards (500)	International	Financial information on companies
Extel International News Cards (501)	International	Company news
Facts on File (265)	International	Short news items
Financial Times (622)	International	Business and financial news
Harvard Business Review (122)	International	Full text of HBR articles
Hoppenstedt Directory of German Companies (529)	Germany	Corporate directory
ICC International Business Research (563)	International	Financial analysts' reports
IDD M&A Transactions (550)	International	Merger and acquisition activity
Industry Data Surveys (189)	International	Information directory
INFOMAT International Business (583)	International	Industry and product news
INVESTEXT (545)	International	Company and industry financial analyses
Japan Economic Newswire (612)	Japan	Business, economic and general news

FIGURE 1: Continued

Database (DIALOG Number)	Geographic Focus	Type of Information
Japan Technology (582)	Japan	Research, technology and business news
Journal of Commerce (637)	International	Trade and transportation information
Knight-Ridder Financial News (609)	International	Financial and business news
KOMPASS Europe (590)	Europe	Corporate directory
KOMPASS UK (591)	United Kingdom	Corporate directory
Management Contents (75)	International	Academic business literature
Moody's Corporate News - International (43)	International	Business and financial news
PAIS International (43)	International	Public policy related topics
PAPERS	International	Full text of several U.S. newspapers
Piers Exports (571,572)	United States	U.S. Export Shipping Records

Piers Exports (573,574)	United States	U.S. Import Shipping Records
PTS International Forecasts (83)	International	Economic and industry forecasts
PTS Marketing & Advertising Reference Service (570)	International	Marketing and advertising information
PTS New Product Announcements (621)	International	New product information
PTS Newsletter Database (636)	International	Economic, social & political trends
PTS PROMT (16)	International	Industry and company information from trade and business journals
Teikoku Databank: Japanese Companies (502)	Japan	Corporate directory, financial information
Trade Names Database (116)	International	Directory of 280,000 brand names & owners

Source: DIALOG Database Catalog 1991. DIALOG Information Services.

93

or for specific products. Any of the databases offering business, economic, social, political or general news are useful for this purpose. However, *PTS PROMT* and *INFOMAT World Business* are particularly valuable here. These are very extensive databases which index and summarize articles from business, trade and professional journals from around the world. Many of these journals are very difficult to find and are not indexed anywhere else. Moreover, article summaries are written in English, though many of the original articles are in other languages. Specialized event and product codes allow searchers to seek general information or target articles on a specific product and/or business function.

Financial analysis assignments require the collection of financial data as well as financial news and analysts' opinions about a company. Many of the corporate directory databases contain limited financial information about the companies they describe. *Extel International Financial Cards* contains more extensive information. Several databases, including *Financial Times, Knight-Ridder Financial News,* and *Moody's Corporate News-International* contain financial news about companies. Two databases, *INVESTEXT* and *ICC International Business Research* contain financial analysts' evaluation of specific companies.

The corporate directory databases are the best sources of information about companies who are potential customers, partners and/or competitors. Students may extract lists of companies by industry, including any selective criteria on size, number of employees and/or geographic presence they deem advisable. Resources include worldwide directories such as *D&B International Dun's Market Identifiers,* and country-specific databases such as the *Hoppenstedt Directory of German Companies* or the *Teikoku Databank: Japanese Companies.*

Competitive analysis research projects require students to identify the major competitors and competitive practices within a global, regional or country-specific industry. In addition, the strategies, plans, strengths and weaknesses of major competitors must also be assessed. All of the databases described thus far may be used in this process. There are others which are also of value in competitive analysis. For example, *Industry Data Surveys* identifies the sources of information available for a particular industry, while

PTS Marketing and Advertising Reference Service indexes articles on marketing and promotional activities of firms in various industries. By identifying all the DIALOG databases that contain information on a particular company, the *DIALOG Company Name Finder* can help locate comprehensive information on a selected competitor.

These examples describe the application of electronic data retrieval techniques to the basic types of research projects in international business education. These techniques may also be used in support of other class activities. Students may use database searches to update or expand the information used in case analysis assignments. These resources may also be used to gather practical examples of course concepts, identify articles for class discussion, or provide background information on firms being studied. Of course, the academic literature databases, *ABI Inform* and *Management Contents,* are invaluable for the traditional research paper assignment.

In short, the databases listed in Figure 1 may be used to support a wide range of learning activities in international business courses with wide access and very reasonable cost.

ADDITIONAL ONLINE AND CD ROM RESOURCES

While the DIALOG databases just discussed can serve the needs of most international business courses, they are not the only resources available. There are numerous additional sources of information which instructors can use for special purposes or to illustrate the breadth of electronic information resources. These resources are cataloged in *Computer-Readable Databases: A Directory and Data Sourcebook,* published by Gale Research Incorporated, also accessible as File 230 on DIALOG. Of the thousands of database either online or in CD ROM form, the following are representative of the resources appropriate for international business education. Contact information for suppliers of all databases cited in this section appears in Figure 2.

For market assessment projects, the general DIALOG databases cited above may be augmented with additional, more specific

FIGURE 2: SUPPLIERS OF INTERNATIONAL BUSINESS DATABASES IN SECTION IV

Centre d'Etudes Prospectives et d'Informations
   Internationales
9, rue Georges Pitard
F-75015 Paris, France
Phone: 01 48426414

Data-Star
Suite 110
485 Devon Park Drive
Wayne, PA 19087
(800) 221-7754

Dow Jones & Company, Inc.
P.O. Box 300
Princeton, NJ 08540-0300
Phone: (609) 520-4000

Mead Data Central (Nexis and Lexis)
9393 Springboro Pike
P.O. Box 933
Dayton, OH 45401
(800) 227-4908

NewsNet, Inc.
945 Haverford Road
Bryn Mawr, PA 19010
(800) 345-1301

S.J. Rundt & Associates
160 E. 63rd St.
New York, NY 10021
Phone: (212) 838-0141

Financial Times Business Information (FTBI)
Financial Times Electronic Publishing
One Southwark Bridge
London SE1 9LS, England
Phone: 071-873 3000

Helsingin Kauppakorkeakoulun Kirjasto
Information Services
Runeberginkatu 22-24
SF-00100 Helsinki 10, Finland
Phone: 0 43131

International Monetary Fund
Washington, D.C. 20431
(202) 623-7430

Standard and Poor's Compustat Services
7400 South Alton Court
Englewood, CO 80112
(800) 525-8640

United Nations Statistical Office
Room DC2-1620
New York, NY 10017
Phone: (212) 963-4996

The World Bank Group
1818 H Street NW
Washington, DC 20433
(202)473-2205

resources from other suppliers. Online resources include *European Community Business Forecasts* (on the NewsNet system) and *Euroscope* (Nexis) for information on EC markets and the 1992 initiative. Information on business conditions and opportunities in the former Soviet Union are contained in *Russia Express* (NewsNet) and *SovData DiaLine* (Nexis). Similar information for the Middle East can be found in *Middle East Business Intelligence* (NewsNet). S. J. Rundt & Associates offers *World Risk Analysis Package* online from Reuters Information Services in Canada, or on diskette from the producer. This database is a proprietary collection of reports on business risk in 61 countries. *United Nations Commodity Trade Statistics* provides comprehensive trade statistics on diskette format and is also available online from Reuters Information Services in Canada. The World Bank also publishes several collections of international statistics in diskette format. Titles in this series include *World Development Indicators, Social Indicators of Development, World Debt Tables* and *African Economic and Financial Data.*

There are several CD ROM resources available for market assessment purposes. The International Monetary Fund offers a comprehensive statistical database, *International Financial Statistics,* at a cost of $1,000 per year to libraries or academic departments and $350 per year to a single academic user. *HELECON on CD ROM* (Helsingin Kauppakorkeakoulun Kirjasto) is a collection of eight databases on European management and business which costs $2,200 per year. It includes collections of statistics, market assessment reports, academic literature, trade literature and business opportunities and resources in Europe. Finally, *CHELEM* (Centre d'Etudes Prospectives et d'Informations Internationales) is a collection of five databases offering historical trade, financial and national income account statistics for several countries at an annual cost of 4,000 FF.

A major resource for the financial analysis of companies is Financial Times Business Information, an online information service in the UK. This firm provides a series of databases with financial information, including *FINSTAT, Financial Times Business Reports: Finance and Business* and *Financial Times Mergers and Acquisitions International.* The major CD ROM resource for financial analysis of companies is *Global Vantage* (Standard and Poor's

Compustat Services). This database provides financial information on over 6,700 companies in 31 countries at an annual subscription rate of $10,000.

In the search for opportunities, support services and/or potential customers, several resources provide important information. Online sources of general information on trade opportunities and support services include *Business Databank* (Data Star), *The International Trade Reporter* (Lexis), and *The Exporter* (NewsNet). Information on more specific opportunities in selected areas of the world is available from sources such as *Russia Express Contracts* (NewsNet), *USSR Business* (NewsNet) and *East Asia Express* (NewsNet). The best CD ROM resource here is the *Global Vantage* system described above.

In a rapidly changing environment, competitive analysis demands access to very current information. For this reason, online applications are more useful for this type of project. Among the available resources are several databases offered by Dow Jones & Company, including *Dow Jones Business and Financial Report, Dow Jones International News* and *DowQuest.* NewsNet offers *The International Information Report* for general coverage and *German Business Scope,* which focuses on the German business scene.

These examples illustrate the wealth of material available to the international business research in electronic form. The list of resources grows daily. While cost is still a barrier for many of the services, international business faculty can select key databases to supplement those available at lower rates through DIALOG's CIP.

CONCLUSIONS

In sum, electronic data retrieval applications remain one of the most underappreciated and underutilized applications of microcomputers in business education. However, the traditional barriers of cost, inaccessibility, and difficulty of use are rapidly falling. Several resources are low in cost and relatively easy to use. These resources make a wide variety of databases available for use in international business education. Several important international business databases may now be used in support of a broad range of student learning activities in international business classes.

REFERENCES

Barcellos, Silvia de Oliveira, August 1990. A project for improving interaction between users and information centers: Public access to databases in Brazil. *Electronic Library*, 224-27.

Bardes, D'Ellen, July/August 1986. Attention novices: Friendly intro to shiny disks. *Library Software Review*, 241-45.

Chen, Ching Chih and David I. Raitt, 1990. How optical products have been used in the U.S. and western Europe. Paper presentation at the National Online Meeting. EDRS Reports.

Cohen, Elaine and Margo Young, November/December 1986. Cost comparison of abstracts and indexes on paper, CD ROM, and online. *Optical Information Systems*, 485-90.

Daniels, Craig E., August 1984. Online information retrieval: An underutilized educational tool. *Information Services and Use*, 229-43.

Desmarais, Norman, May 1986. Laser libraries: Publishers are providing information on optical disks. *BYTE*, 235-46.

_____ December 1986. Buying and selling laserbases. *Electronic and Optical Publishing Review*, 184-88.

Doney, Lloyd D. and Steven C. Ross, February 1987. A set of basic computing capabilities for undergraduate business students. *Journal of Education for Business*, 215-217.

Drucker, Peter, June 5, 1985. Playing in the information based 'orchestra.' *Wall Street Journal*.

Dyer, Robert F., Summer 1987. An integrated design for personal computers in the marketing curriculum. *Journal of the Academy of Marketing Science*, 15; 10-15.

Edyburn, Dave L., Summer 1988. Examining the successful retrieval of information by students using online databases. *School Library Media Quarterly*, 256-59.

Ekwurzel, Drucilla and Bernard Saffran, December 1985. Online information retrieval for economists: the Economic Literature Index. *Journal of Economic Literature*, 1728-1763.

Helgerson, Linda W., Summer 1986. CD ROM search and retrieval software: The requirements and the realities. *Library Hi Tech*, 69-77.

Kurtz, David L. and Louis E. Boone, Summer 1987. The current status of microcomputer usage in the marketing programs of AACSB-accredited colleges and universities. *Journal of the Academy of Marketing Science*, 10-15.

Johnson, Charles M., 1989. Online corporate intelligence in marketing research courses. *Proceedings*. American Marketing Association Microcomputers in the Marketing Curriculum Conference, 66-73.

Lambert, Steve and Suzanne Ropiequet, eds., 1986. *CD ROM: The New Papyrus: The Current and Future State of the Art*. Redmond, WA: Microsoft Press.

Large, Andrew J., August 1990. The foreign language barrier and electronic information. *Online Review*, 251-66.

Laub, Leonard, May 1986. The evolution of mass storage. *BYTE,* 161-72.

Luhn, Robert, April 1987. PC World CD ROM forum: CD ROM goes to work. *PC World,* 220-31.

McGinty, Tony, March 1986. Text crunching: Publishers squeeze volumes onto laser read disks. *Electronic Learning,* 22-26.

Miller, Fred, Fall 1985. Integrating the personal computer into the marketing curriculum: A programmatic outline. *Journal of Marketing Education,* 7-11.

Miller, Fred, May 1989. Integrating electronic information retrieval techniques into the business classroom. *Journal of Education for Business,* 376-80.

Miller, Fred, 1989. Suggestions for using DIALOG's CIP in Seven Marketing Courses. *Proceedings.* American Marketing Association Microcomputers in the Marketing Curriculum Conference, 59-65.

Miller, Tim, March/April 1987. Competitive intelligence: Staying alive in the jungle. *Online Access Guide,* 44-52.

Nace, Ted, February 1986. Lighting a path to the future. *Macworld,* 100-6.

Nicholls, Paul and Shaheen Majid, August 1989. The potential for CD-ROM technology in less-developed countries. *Canadian Library Journal,* 257-63.

O'Connor, Mary Ann, July/August 1986. Education and CD ROM. *Optical Information Systems,* 329-31.

O'Leary, Mick, September 1986. DIALOG Business Connection: DIALOG for the end user. *Online,* 15-24.

Oley, Elizabeth, April 1989. Information retrieval in the classroom. *Journal of Reading,* 590-97.

Plant, Mark W., September 23, 1991. The National Trade Data Bank: A one-year perspective. *Business America,* 2-5.

Salton, Gerard, September 1987. Historical note: The past thirty years in information retrieval. *Journal of the American Society for Information Science,* 375-80.

Sehr, Barbara K., November 1, 1986. High noon for CD ROM. *Datamation,* 79-88.

Spickard, Jim, April 1987. Information please?: Getting facts online. *Profiles,* 20-27.

Thompson, N. J., May 1989. DIALOGLINK and TRADEMARKSCAN-FEDERAL: Pioneers in online images. *Online,* 15-26.

Whieldon, David, December 2, 1986. Look at optical storage. *Computer Decisions,* 58-60.

Wiley, Gale, Summer 1989. On-line references become available through CD ROMs. *Journalism Educator,* 67-68.

Zoellick, Bill, May 1986. CD-ROM software development. *BYTE,* 177-88.

Using International Financial Databases in Teaching International Accounting Courses

Abdel M. Agami

Several international financial databases have become available in recent years that can be accessed by researchers and educators. These financial databases vary significantly as to the countries they cover. Some are international, i.e., include databases from many countries; others are regional, i.e., include corporations from Europe, Asia, Latin America, etc.; still others include only a national coverage, i.e., US corporations, UK corporations, etc. They also vary as to the type of information they make available, i.e., complete financial statements, selected items from the financial statements, market prices, financial ratios, etc. They also vary as to the frequency of updating the information; some update information annually, others quarterly, monthly, weekly, or daily. They also vary as to the medium in which the information is provided; some of the services provide the information in hard copies, others provide it in the form of a datadisk, some provide online services, etc. Choi provides a detailed inventory of such services [Choi, 1988].

Abdel M. Agami is Professor of Accounting at Old Dominion University in Norfolk, VA 23529.

[Haworth co-indexing entry note]: "Using International Financial Databases in Teaching International Accounting Courses." Agami, Abdel M. Co-published simultaneously in the *Journal of Teaching in International Business* (The Haworth Press, Inc.) Vol. 4, No. 3/4, 1993, pp. 103-113; and: *Utilizing New Information Technology in Teaching of International Business: A Guide for Instructors* (ed: Fahri Karakaya and Erdener Kaynak) The Haworth Press, Inc., 1993, pp. 103-113. Multiple copies of this article/chapter may be purchased from The Haworth Document Delivery Center. Call 1-800-3-HAWORTH (1-800-342-9678) between 9:00 - 5:00 (EST) and ask for DOCUMENT DELIVERY CENTER.

103

The purpose of this article is to illustrate how to use these data-bases in teaching international accounting courses, and to point out the advantages of such use.

INTERNATIONAL ACCOUNTING COURSES

There has been a steady increase in the number of business schools offering international accounting courses at the undergraduate and/or graduate level in the last twenty years [Mueller, 1965; Seidler, 1967; Bomeli, 1969; Rueschhoff, 1972; Kubin, 1973; Dascher, 1973; Ameiss, 1974; Schoenfeld, 1974; Brummet, 1975; Foutz, 1975; Clay, 1975; Burns, 1979; Pearson et al., 1980; Mintz, 1980; Agami, 1983; Foroughi, 1987; Sherman, 1987; Stout & Schweikart, 1989; Agami, 1991; Huang & Mintz, 1992].

Professors teaching international accounting for the first time, as well as those revising their courses, have to make decisions about such concerns as topics to be covered, time to be allocated to each topic, grouping of topics into meaningful sections. Several studies have ranked topics covered in international accounting courses based on the importance of these topics in the views of academicians and practitioners [Dascher, 1973; Burns, 1979; Mintz, 1980; Scott & Troberg, 1980; Agami, 1983; Foroughi, 1987; Sherman, 1987; Stout & Schweikart, 1989; Agami, 1991; Huang & Mintz, 1992]. All these studies indicate the following topics as being important: foreign currency translation; the role and development of international accounting standards; harmonization of accounting standards in various countries; taxation of multinational enterprises; the study of the impact of inflation on the financial results of multinational enterprises; financial disclosure of global enterprises; information related to management of the operations of global enterprises; and issues and problems related to auditing of multinational enterprises.

The ranking of foreign currency translation as an important topic is understandable. The adoption of the floating rate system by most free economy countries, the increase in the volatility of foreign exchange rates, and the existence of a number of alternative accounting methods for translating financial statements have made foreign currency translation one of the most important and controversial issues in international accounting.

Also ranked high are the development of international accounting standards and the efforts toward harmonization of the differences in accounting and auditing standards between countries. This may be attributed to the growth of multinational enterprises that operate in various countries and consequently have to comply with the accounting and auditing standards of these countries. Also, harmonization of these standards enhances the ability of the international investor to screen profitable investments in various countries.

The high ranking of accounting for inflation does not come as a surprise to anyone. The inflation rate was very high in the last few years, and varied drastically from one country to another. Without a proper accounting for inflation, the international investor faces the risk of not getting an adequate return on the investment, or even losing the original investment.

Topics related to management of the operations of multinational enterprises such as financing and investing, financial risk management, performance evaluation, transfer pricing, etc., were ranked fairly high; this indicates that a significant portion of the international accounting course is devoted to the accounting problems of multinational enterprises.

The author groups the above topics into two sections: a section entitled "financial reporting issues encountered by multinational enterprises," and a section entitled "the internal problems and issues facing multinational enterprises in planning, controlling, and evaluating their operations." The author adds to these two sections a third section entitled "comparative studies of accounting standards and practices in selected countries."

The first section, dealing with financial reporting problems, includes topics such as accounting for the translation of foreign transactions and financial statements from foreign currencies to domestic currencies, and considers the conceptual basis for choosing a particular method of translation. Also contained in this section are accounting for inflation in various countries, and the issue of whether MNEs should translate the financial statements of their foreign subsidiaries and branches from foreign currencies first and then restate these translated financial statements for the domestic inflation, or whether they should restate the financial statements of those subsidiaries and branches for local foreign inflation and then translate them from foreign currencies to domestic currencies. Some other topics referred to include consolidation of foreign subsidiaries, segmental disclosure of foreign operations, and social responsibility disclosure of multinational enterprises.

The second section is devoted to the development of accounting information needed by the management of the MNE in planning and controlling international operations. Included are such topics as: evaluating foreign investment proposals; determining the most economic financing outlets; minimizing financial risk associated with investments in different parts of the world and different currencies; evaluating the performance of foreign branches, subsidiaries and their respective managers; establishing equitable transfer prices for goods or services exchanged among affiliates; and the principles of foreign and domestic taxation of international operations.

The third section is concerned with the study of accounting and auditing standards and practices of selected foreign countries and regions such as Europe, Canada, Central and South America, Australia and New Zealand, socialist countries, and developing countries. The purpose for studying these countries is to identify similarities and differences between accounting standards and practices of those countries and those of the USA. Appendix 1 presents the organization of the international accounting course and the topics covered in the course by the author.

The only study that investigated the methods of instruction in teaching the international accounting course was the one made by Agami in 1983. This study found that lecturing was used in teaching the international accounting course in all the cases investigated (100%), term papers were required from students in only 74% of the cases studied, the case method of instruction was used 52%, oral presentation by students was used 47%, and independent projects submitted by students in only 39% of the cases studied [Agami, 1983, p. 73].

The number of cases developed for use in teaching international accounting is still very small. A good source of cases is the Harvard Business School Case Services. The use of cases to supplement lectures is, in the author's opinion, a very effective method for teaching international accounting due to the complex environment in which international business is conducted and in which MNEs operate. In addition to simulating real world situations, the case method arouses students' interest and generates more student participation and interaction. Independent projects assigned to students allow them to research areas of particular interest to them, such as the accounting standards and practices of a specific country or the reporting problems of a particular multinational enterprise or industry. These projects serve two desirable purposes: to stimulate the intellectual ability of students and encourage their independent thinking; and to enrich our library on international accounting.

USE OF INTERNATIONAL FINANCIAL DATABASES IN INTERNATIONAL ACCOUNTING COURSES

As was mentioned in the preceding section of this article and in Appendix 1, the third part of the international accounting course which the author teaches includes a survey of the accounting standards and corporate financial reporting practices in selected foreign countries. The objective of this part of the course is to give students an opportunity to identify similarities and differences in cultural, economic, business, and accounting standards and practices of the US and other countries.

Each student chooses a foreign country that he or she is interested in. The student also chooses a corporation that is domiciled in the foreign country and a similar US corporation. The student then researches the cultural, economic, business, and accounting standards of this country and the accounting practices of the corporation. The student then compares the cultural, economic, business, and accounting standards of this foreign country and the accounting practices of the corporation with those of the US and the US corporation. The student is required to state whether the differences in accounting standards and practices between the two countries have hindered the student's analysis in any respect and what are the student's views as to how to overcome those national barriers.

The computerized financial database that the author uses is DIS-CLOSURE/WORLDSCOPE. The most recent edition of this software provides access to the financial data of about 7000 companies in over 25 countries (see Appendix 2 for a list of the countries) and over 24 industries. The data for each company is presented in standardized format. The financial data is available for ten years (five years of displayable data). The record of each company contains 500 data fields (see Appendix 3 for a summary of the data). The data is updated monthly. Retrieved data can be displayed, printed, or transferred to disk. This is a very important feature; it allows students to transfer whatever data they need onto their own disk for whatever analysis they want to do on another computer. This way they do not tie up the computer on which the DISCLOSURE/WORLDSCOPE disk is stored so that other students can use it. It is also a very useful feature for the instructor for grading purposes. The author requires the students to submit a copy of the disk where they saved the data and their analysis along with the final written report. Generally the final report consists of four sections. The first section provides general information about the country chosen by the student such as geographical information about the country, the political system, the population, the language, culture, economy, etc. The second section contains information about the business environment, accounting and auditing standards and practices of the country, and status of the accounting profession in the country. The third section includes a study of financial reporting practices and the financial performance of a corporation domiciled in the country. The fourth section presents the student's observations and remarks as to similarities and differences in cultural, economic, business, and accounting standards and practices of the US and other countries.

The author has required students to do the financial part of the project using hard copy financial sources such as Annual Reports, 10-K, Moody's Industrial, etc., in the past years. Recently a computerized financial database, namely DISCLOSURE/WORLDSCOPE became available for gathering the data needed for this project. The author has found that the use of computerized financial databases reduces the time the student spends on collecting and processing data and computing certain ratios, gives students more time for analysis, interpretation, and inference without increasing the total time spent on the project. It also encourages students to increase the horizon over which they analyze the performance of the company, and gives students more self-confidence in use of the computer and state-of-the-art information technology.

REFERENCES

Agami, Abdel M., "The International Accounting Course: State of the Art." *Journal of Accounting Education* (Fall 1983), pp. 67-77.

Agami, Abdel M., "Adding International Dimension to the Accounting Curriculum." *Journal of Teaching in International Business* (Vol. 3, No. 2, 1991), pp. 53-63.

Ameiss, Albert P., "International Accounting at the Senior Student Level." *International Journal of Accounting* (Fall 1974), pp. 107-121.

Bomeli, Edwin C., "Curricular Recognition of International Accounting–An Appraisal." *International Journal of Accounting* (Fall 1969), pp. 85-96.

Brummet, R. Lee, "Internationalism and the Future of Accounting Education." *International Journal of Accounting* (Fall 1975), pp. 161-165.

Burns, Jane O., "A Study of International Accounting Education in the United States." *International Journal of Accounting* (Fall 1979), pp. 135-145.

Choi, Frederick D.S., "International Data Sources for Empirical Research in Financial Management." *Financial Management* (Summer 1988), pp. 80-98.

Clay, Alvin A., "Undergraduate International Accounting Education." *International Journal of Accounting* (Fall 1975), pp. 187-192.

Dascher, Paul, C.H. Smith, and R.H. Strawser, "Accounting Curriculum Implications of the MNC." *International Journal of Accounting* (Fall 1973), pp. 81-97.

Foroughi, Tahirih, and Barbara Reed, "A Survey of the Present and Desirable International Accounting Topics in Accounting Education." *International Journal of Accounting* (Fall 1987), pp. 69-82.

Foutz, Paul B., "The Teaching of International Accounting." *Management Accounting* (June 1975), pp. 31-33.

Huang, Jiunn C., and Steven M. Mintz, "International Accounting Education: A Global Perspective." *The Accounting Educators' Journal* (Vol. IV, No. 1), pp. 69-85.

Kubin, Konrad W., "The Changing Nature of International Accounting Courses." *International Journal of Accounting* (Fall 1973), pp. 99-111.

Mintz, Steven M., "Internationalization of the Accounting Curriculum." *International Journal of Accounting* (Fall 1980), pp. 137-151.

Mueller, Gerhard G., "Whys and Hows of International Accounting." *Accounting Review* (April 1965), pp. 386-394.

Pearson, Michael A., John K. Ryan, and Lorraine J. Hicks, "Internationalizing the Accounting Curriculum." *Massachusetts CPA Review* (Nov.-Dec. 1980), pp. 29-30.

Rueschhoff, Norlin G., "The Undergraduate International Accounting Course." *Accounting Review* (October 1972), pp. 833-836.

Schoenfeld, Hans, "International Influences on the Contemporary Accounting Curriculum: International Accounting Instruction at the University of Illinois at Urbana-Champaign." *International Journal of Accounting* (Fall 1974), pp. 71-85.

Scott, George M., and P. Troberg, *Eighty-Eight International Accounting Problems in Rank Order of Importance–A Delphi Evaluation.* Sarasota, FL: American Accounting Association, 1980.

Seidler, Lee J., "International Accounting–The Ultimate Theory Course." *Accounting Review* (October 1967), pp. 775-781.
Sherman, W. Richard, "Internationalizing the Accounting Curriculum." *Journal of Accounting Education* (Fall 1987), pp. 259-275.
Stout, David E., and James A. Schweikart, "The Relevance of International Accounting to the Accounting Curriculum: A Comparison of Practitioner and Educator Opinion." *Issues in Accounting Education* (Spring 1989), pp. 126-143.

APPENDIX 1

INTERNATIONAL ACCOUNTING

Hours

INTRODUCTION   3

SECTION I: External Accounting Information
Needs of Multinational Enterprises   9-15

1. Consolidation of foreign subsidiaries
2. Accounting problems related to the existence of different accounting standards in different countries
3. Accounting problems related to different currencies in different countries
4. Accounting problems related to different rates of inflation in different countries
5. Financial, social, and environmental disclosures required in different countries
6. Problems related to the existence of different auditing standards and practices in different countries

SECTION II: Internal Accounting Information
Needs of Global Enterprises   9-15

1. Information needed for investing and financing overseas
2. Information needed for risk management
3. Information needed for evaluating the performance of foreign subsidiaries
4. Information needed for establishing transfer prices among decentralized subsidiaries of the global enterprise
5. Information needed for minimizing taxes

Hours

SECTION III: A Comparative Study of
Accounting and Auditing Standards in
Selected Countries   9-15

North America
Europe
Central and South America
Australia and New Zealand
Pacific Rim Countries
Developing Countries
Socialist Countries ?

45

APPENDIX 2

COUNTRIES INCLUDED IN
DISCLOSURE/WORLDSCOPE

1. Australia
2. Austria
3. Belgium
4. Canada
5. Denmark
6. Finland
7. France
8. Germany
9. Hong Kong
10. Ireland
11. Italy
12. Japan
13. South Korea
14. Malaysis
15. Mexico
16. Netherlands
17. New Zealand
18. Norway
19. Singapore
20. South Africa
21. Spain
22. Sweden
23. Switzerland
24. United Kingdom
25. United States

APPENDIX 3

SUMMARY OF DATA INCLUDED IN DISCLOSURE/WORLDSCOPE

RESUME DATA:

Name	Stock Exchange(s)
Address	Stock Indices
Telephone	Ticker Symbol
Business Description	CUSIP Number
SIC Codes	SEDOL Number
Number of Employees	VALOR Number
Currency	ISIN Number
Exchange Rates	Current Outstanding Shares
Auditor	Number of Shareholders
Auditor's Opinion	

FINANCIAL DATA: Unless otherwise noted, all data is available from 1980 to the present.

Annual Income Statements
Annual Balance Sheets (Assets/Liabilities)
Supplementary Financials including loan, debt and other line items
Sources of Funds
Uses of Funds
Proceeds from Sale/Issuance of stock
Ratios–Annual
Ratios–Five Year Averages: 1984 to the present
Annual Growth Rates
Five Year Growth Rates: 1984 to the present

STOCK DATA: Unless otherwise noted, all data is available from 1980 to the present.

U.S. and Non-U.S. Stock Price/Trading Data
Stock Performance Data
U.S. Interim Share Data
Non-U.S. Interim Share Data: 1989 to the present
U.S. Month End Market Prices: 1985 to the present

Non-U.S. Month End Market Prices: 1987 to the present
Annual Stock Statistics
Five Year Stock Averages

TEXTUAL DATA:

Accounting Practices Abstracts
Financial Footnote Abstracts
Key Officers and Titles

Evaluation of Computer Based Information Sources for International Business

Richard K. Harper
Ronald F. Bush

SUMMARY. Faculty struggle to keep abreast of quick-paced technological change which has generated an unprecedented number of computer-based information sources. Four such sources are evaluated by students/faculty of the undergraduate International Business course. An on-line library catalogue system; Infotrac; the National Trade Data Bank (NTDB) and a recent simulation, providing export information, *Export To Win!* are evaluated. Student open-ended evaluations are content analyzed by the authors and the results of a survey rating the sources on four criteria are reported. Suggestions are provided to aid teachers of International Business to effectively and efficiently integrate computer data sources into their course.

Richard K. Harper, PhD, is Assistant Professor and Ronald F. Bush, PhD, is Professor at the University of West Florida.

Address correspondence to: Dr. Ronald F. Bush, Department of Marketing, College of Business, University of West Florida, Pensacola, FL 32514.

[Haworth co-indexing entry note]: "Evaluation of Computer Based Information Sources for International Business." Harper, Richard K., and Ronald F. Bush. Co-published simultaneously in the *Journal of Teaching in International Business* (The Haworth Press, Inc.) Vol. 4, No. 3/4, 1993, pp. 115-134; and: *Utilizing New Information Technology in Teaching of International Business: A Guide for Instructors* (ed: Fahri Karakaya and Erdener Kaynak) The Haworth Press, Inc., 1993, pp. 115-134. Multiple copies of this article/chapter may be purchased from The Haworth Document Delivery Center. Call 1-800-3-HAWORTH (1-800-342-9678) between 9:00 - 5:00 (EST) and ask for DOCUMENT DELIVERY CENTER.

115

INTRODUCTION

With little doubt the last decade has seen unprecedented change in the internationalization of college of business curricula. Sweeping world change has brought globalization of the economy to the forefront of curriculum design. Much of this change has been implemented as a result of university faculty recognizing the need to internationalize the curriculum (Hawkins, 1984). For others, accreditation societies such as the AACSB have issued mandates requiring consideration of the international issues in degree programs (Evans and Skadden, 1990, p. 14; Nehrt, 1987 and Thanopoulos, 1987). Regardless of the source of the change, the fact is that internationalization of business school curricula is a prominent force today and undoubtedly will continue to increase in importance in the future.

A concurrent sweeping change affecting business school curricula has been the development of and increasing availability of computer based information sources. It is estimated that there are over 3,000 data bases available today and 200 to 300 of them apply to business (Churchill, 1991, p. 261). Data bases are usually defined by the type of information they contain. Bibliographic data bases, for example, provide references to magazine and journal articles. There are data bases which provide (a) company information (*Standard and Poor's Corporate Descriptions* and *Moody's Corporate Profiles*); (b) directories of company information (*D&B Dun's Market Identifiers* and *Standard and Poor's Corporate Directory*); (c) information on government contracts (*Commerce Business Daily* and *DMS Contract Awards*); (d) economic and demographic information (*Cendata* and *PTS U.S. Forecasts*) among others. There is an excellent explanation of how to use computerized data bases in Johnson, Faria and Maier (1984).

With quick-paced changes in computer technology, faculty struggle to keep up with the ever increasing information concerning what sources of information are available, their information content, as well as the operational characteristics of these sources. The purpose of this article, therefore, is to provide (a) a description of four computer information sources that may be useful to teachers of International Business and (b) an evaluation of each source in terms of its suitability for use in the International Business course by students.

OVERVIEW OF SELECTED COMPUTER BASED
INFORMATION RESOURCES

For the purposes of this study the authors selected four computer based sources of information. As noted above, there are many computer data bases and certainly many others should be considered for evaluation. The rationale for evaluating the four sources evaluated here was that they do cover several of the various types, or formats, of computerized sources available and they are typical of the sources that many teachers of International Business might consider. The sources selected for evaluation were: (a) an on-line library catalogue system (*LUIS, Library User Information Service*) which is very similar in operation to many university's systems; (b) *Infotrac* (Information Access Company), a CD-ROM based index of journal publications; (c) *National Trade Data Bank (NTDB)*(U.S. Department of Commerce), a source of export-relevant information from the U.S. Department of Commerce; and (d) *Export To Win!* (Strategic Management Group, Inc.), a simulation providing information on exporting goods. It is important to note that *Export To Win!* is not a typical simulation which just requires students to input decisions and receive standardized result reports. In addition to this, students are provided with the information necessary for them to make any one of a myriad of decisions required to export goods. Hence, the authors consider this simulation as an information "source" as well as a simulation. Each of the four information sources is described in the following paragraphs. (Note: the authors provide a more detailed explanation of *Export To Win!* since it is both unique and not likely to be immediately accessible in the reader's library.)

LUIS (On-Line Catalog)

The Library User Information Service (LUIS) is not unlike the many computerized catalogue systems in States having university systems. LUIS gives the user information regarding all catalogued collections in some 13 library systems in the authors' State University System. It can be searched by author, title, subject or keyword (keyword searches may employ logical connectors). The service will give bibliographic, location and holdings information, as well as telling the user whether materials are charged out (giving the due date), on reserve, in process, or missing.

Infotrac

The Infotrac CD-ROM database available at the authors' University contains both the Academic Library Edition and the Business Index. The Academic Library Edition provides bibliographic references to over 1100 scholarly and general interest journals. The Business Index indexes over 800 business, management and trade journals, including the *Wall Street Journal* and *New York Times*. Abstracts are provided for about 150 major management and computer journals. CD-ROM updates are provided monthly.

Access to the database normally is through an extensive menu system, where students first enter keywords and then select from a list of subheadings generated for that keyword. Students may then view abstracts and/or bibliographic citations under that subheading and print desired references. More selective searches can be performed by using logical connectors between keywords in the "expanded search" mode.

National Trade Data Bank (NTDB)

The CD-ROM edition of the NTDB contains trade promotion and international economic data from 15 Federal agencies, including CIA, Federal Reserve System, Ex-Im Bank, Overseas Private Investment Corporation, several branches of the Department of Commerce, and more. One CD-ROM contains about 100,000 documents selected for their potential relevance to international commerce. Among these reports were:

- *Market Research Reports*–includes *Country Marketing Plans, Industry Sector Analyses* and *Foreign Economic Trends.* These are indispensable aids to any international business research assignment.
- *Business America*–Commerce's bi-weekly publication that is designed to help American companies sell overseas.

- *A Basic Guide to Exporting*–a comprehensive introduction with references to detailed information.
- *Trade Opportunity Program*–sales opportunities and leads from U.S. embassies abroad.

Each CD-ROM comes with files containing access software and user manuals. There are two basic modes of access. The Browse mode lets inexperienced users search by source, topic, program, subject or item. Once materials are retrieved, selected documents may be downloaded to diskette for later use, or they may be examined on-screen, or both (all materials are ASCII textfiles). A more powerful, but more complex, logical search capability is provided for more experienced users. Most searches are very fast, using only several seconds to generate lists of dozens of documents.

Export To Win!

Export To Win! is a recent (1991) computer simulation developed to aid students understand the exporting process. Therefore, it may be thought of as an ancillary in International Business classes. The simulation was developed by SMG in association with the Port Authority of New York and New Jersey. It is distributed by the College Division, South-Western Publishing Company, Cincinnati, Ohio.

Learning Objectives

The learning objectives for the simulation are to:

1. Learn that exporting makes good business sense; a company with an export focus can increase sales and profits and compete better domestically;
2. Learn about the importance of research and developing an international marketing plan; locating and selecting markets and creating a distribution network as well as arranging financing to get started are all required of students;
3. Discover how proper export management will permit global marketing; students learn how competitive marketing mixes allow success in international markets.

Setting

A student player is cast as the marketing manager for Xebec, an industrial manufacturer desiring to export its products. The marketing manager must analyze target markets, and put together a distribution network, and negotiate international pricing decisions. Dozens of decisions are made over a simulated five year period. Students' performances are reviewed in an ongoing fashion; and they receive strategy suggestions as well as a large quantity of decision aiding information. They are also given directions to seek other resources to aid in their export planning. Results are displayed on Xebec's income statement.

A manufacturer of industrial process control equipment, Xebec markets two products in the U.S.; a complete "system," (the System 200) and components for the system (the System 100). The System 200 has an ex-factory price of $3,924.04 and the System 100 components cost $481.78 each. Annual sales are $13.5 million and students begin the simulation by receiving a memo from the CEO asking them to take charge of Xebec's international efforts. Students are prompted as to whether they want to "start," "learn about their competition," or "seek information sources." There are "learning prompts" throughout the simulation. For example, if a student wishes to "start" the simulation without learning anything about their competition, they are allowed to do so but not without the prompt "teaching" them that they are about to make a mistake and that it makes good business sense to learn as much about competition as possible.

Decision Areas

Students are given a general set of goals for each of the five years of the simulation. In *Year 1*, the primary objective is to learn about sources of information for exporting. Students are introduced to the services provided by the Chamber of Commerce and Department of Commerce, among others. They are introduced to the notions of Export Trading Companies, Joint Ventures, Licensing, and the World Bank.

In *Year 2*, students learn about internal decision alternatives.

Pricing–they learn concepts such as Base Price, Ex-Factory/Ex-Works Price, Free Alongside a Ship, Import Licensing, Sight Draft, and Time Draft. *Export Licensing*–students are introduced to Bureau of Export Administration, Commodity Control List, General License GTE, Project License, and Service Supply License. *Financing*–if customers want or need financing students learn about Financing Programs; Commodity Credit Corporation, Department of Agriculture, Foreign Credit Insurance Association, Letters of Credit, Telex Money Transfer, and the Working Capital Guarantee Program. *Shipping*–students learn about Consolidation, Containerization, Customs Brokers, Freight Forwarding, and the Transportation Telephone Tickler. *Insurance*–to guard against goods that may be damaged en route, students are introduced to Contingency Insurance, Open Policy, and Valued Basis Insurance.

In *Year 3*, the CEO directs the student to establish a full-fledged export department. *Internal Development*–students must make decisions regarding Agents, Distributors, Trade Directories, New Product Information Services, Trade Journals, and Voice of America. *Market Research*–students are allowed to purchase marketing research information from public and private organizations and learn to use their reports and on-line data bases. They are introduced to the Bureau of the Census, N.E.C. and N.S.P.F. *Distribution Network*–students are asked to plan an overseas distribution network and are introduced to Direct Exporting. *Export Management Company*–the CEO asks the student to use one. Obviously, then the students must learn what an Export Management Company is and how it can help Xebec's export operations.

By *Year 4*, students need to travel to visit the overseas customers. They learn about *Travel & Culture*–they are introduced to the International Travel Certificate and Visa. *Currency Exchange*–students learn to attempt to minimize exchange losses. They learn about Buy-backs, Countertrade, Factoring, Hedging, Inflation, and Receivables. The CEO also requests that the students prepare a *Market Plan.*

In *Year 5*, students are required to develop a *Strategic Plan.* Specifically, students learn about *Product Development*–and the Product Life Cycle. *Tracking Trends*–allows students to learn about the importance of environmental monitoring. They are introduced to organizations and information sources that aid them in the task of identifying market trends. Finally, students are asked to summarize what has worked for Xebec since exporting began. They learn how successful *Global Strategies* for the future incorporate the concepts of *Market Share and Value-Based Goods and Services.*

Hardware Requirements

You need an IBM PC or compatible with at least 640K RAM in order to run *Export To Win!* The simulation runs with either a hard disk or a dual floppy drive system. While the program runs with a monochrome monitor, it is designed to run with a color monitor. Installing the program is very easy; instructions are simple and are contained on the first pages of the student manual. Installation procedures take less than 5 minutes.

Student Manual

The student manual for *Export To Win!* summarizes their yearly objectives and new terms and concepts they are to be introduced to each year. The manual also contains quizzes for each year of operation. A glossary of terms as well as a list of resources and references is also provided in the instructor's manual. Considering the amount of information contained in the manual, it is concise and well-written. It should serve as an aid, rather than a hindrance, to get students truly interested and motivated to compete in the simulation.

METHODS OF EVALUATION

Students in two sections of the course, Business in the International Environment, were asked to compare and evaluate the four computer resources assigned in conjunction with the course. The major goal which student groups sought to accomplish was completion of a research project in which the group assumed a corporate/product identity and developed plans to penetrate a foreign market. The class grade for each student thus depended upon efficient use of available research resources, both computerized and traditional.

Students in the International Business course are typically

introduced to available computerized and traditional resources during an in-class session with the University's business reference librarian early in the semester. This session includes demonstration, using a projection screen, of the resources most likely to be accessed by students in their research. Among these are three of the previously described information sources: LUIS; Infotrac; and the NTDB. Finally, although it is not part of the library based resources, *Export To Win!* was assigned in this course. The in-class session with the Business Reference Librarian also includes an introduction to the traditional (hard copy and microform) international business collection.

The Term Assignment

Each student group was to choose two countries for a comparative market analysis. Restrictions regarding choice of countries were that they must be non-English speaking and not part of the U.S. or its protectorates. The countries were also required to be on different continents. Selection by groups of homogeneous industrial products was discouraged. In each country, the students were to think of themselves as market researchers. They were asked to prepare reports to management with the goal of providing information for management decision making about potential entry into this geographic market with their particular product or service.

Following the introductory session with the Business Reference Librarian, the first assignment has students access NTDB and download market research reports to diskette for 20 countries of their choice. This assignment serves to familiarize them with both the mechanics and substance of the NTDB collection. An additional benefit is that groups become aware of some of the Department of Commerce's recommended possibilities in each of the 20 potential markets, helping eliminate possible bad product/service choices.

Their written reports are required to be submitted in two parts, at different times in the semester. Part I consists of the initial data collection/market assessment effort. In this part of the report, students present relevant information on cultural, economic, marketing, political and competitive factors regarding their product in two countries. Part II consists of the actual plan for entry into the more favorable of the two markets. The Part II report contains an executive summary, a comparative analysis of the two initial markets and a strategy which includes elements of objectives and organization, regulation, investment, financing, forecasts, management, marketing and other relevant factors.

Methods of Evaluation: Content Analysis and Survey

The Term Assignment provided the students with the opportunity to assess the usefulness of the computerized information sources. Two separate measurements were made. First, as part of their group project, students were asked to assess the sources which they had accessed during the course. Specifically, students were asked to provide a written professional review. The authors then conducted a content analysis of these reports and sorted student evaluative statements into positive, negative or neutral categories. Each of the authors conducted the content analysis (interjudge reliability score = .92).

Secondly, after the completion of the course, students were administered a telephone survey in which they were asked additional questions regarding their evaluations of the four computerized information sources. During the telephone survey students were asked to allocate points to each of the four information sources in terms of how well each information source met each of the following criteria:

a. ease of use;
b. effectiveness in aiding the completing of the class project;
c. ability to enhance student's general knowledge of international business, and;
d. the importance that should be placed on the information source in the course in the future.

A total of 14 different student teams, representing 70 students, provided the evaluations. A description of each information source as well as the results of the evaluations follow.

RESULTS

Evaluation 1: Content Analysis of Students' Written Evaluations

Table 1 depicts the content analysis results for all four information sources (see bottom of Table for explanation of the "Evaluation Index").

LUIS. The LUIS (on-line catalog) system was used by only half of the groups. This reflects both the specificity and timeliness of the information required for the term project, and the availability of superior, product- and country-specific resources. Useful information that could be obtained in the library traditional collection typically was limited to general demographic, political and cultural indicators. Information about particular markets within a given country generally was not available or up-to-date in the traditional collection. The authors suspect that this will be the case at most institutions. However, three of the groups that used LUIS had an evaluation index of 1.00 (all positive statements). In these cases, students found that the NTDB complemented and extended the materials referenced in LUIS by providing market specific information. Therefore, LUIS information, when used in conjunction with NTDB information, was viewed as useful to the students.

When evaluating LUIS against the three other information sources, it is the least valuable of the computerized tools for conducting business research. Typical *positive comments* included:

- *large volume of materials,*
- *key word searching eliminated extraneous materials,*
- *quick and easy,*
- *gives a listing for materials found at other universities [in the state system],*
- *far superior to the old card catalog,*
- *gives call number and whether book is checked out.*

Typical *negative comments* included:

- *references are out of date,*
- *general in nature,*
- *limited information on source material.*

Table 1. STUDENT EVALUATIONS OF COMPUTERIZED INFORMATION SOURCES
UTILIZED TO TEACH INTERNATIONAL BUSINESS

| STUDENT | | EVALUATION INDEXES[a] | | |
TEAM	LUIS	INFOTRAC	NTDB	EXPORT TO WIN
1	.66	0	.75	.57
2	na	1	.8	.57
3	1	1	1	.67
4	.33	.5	1	.71
5	na	1	1	.59
6	0	0	1	1
7	.66	.8	.66	1
8	0	0	0	.73
9	0	.5	1	.73
10	0	na	.63	.86
11	1	1	1	.33
12	0	0	0	.43
13	0	0	1	1
14	1	.5	.6	.59

[a]Explanation of the Evaluation Index: Each student team was asked to provide a written analysis of each computerized information source. The authors read the analyses and coded comments as either "positive" or "negative" (neutral comments were not coded). The "evaluation index" was computed as the proportion of positive comments to the total of positive and negative comments. Therefore, an index of .5 means that the number of positive comments equalled the number of negative comments. Any number greater than .5 means the evaluation was more positive than negative; an index less than .5 means the evaluation was more negative than positive. An index of 1.00, of course meant that all the comments were positive. An evaluation where all comments were negative is given a value of zero.

Infotrac. Infotrac was used by over two thirds of the groups. Overall, students offered more positive than negative comments (see Table 1). Again, students found that for performing the class term assignment, the coverage of Infotrac indexed materials tended to be less specific than could be found in the NTDB.

Typical *positive comments* made regarding Infotrac included:

- *nice complement to NTDB–after determining best prospects, used Infotrac to access articles on corporate experiences in these markets*
- *easy to use, saves time*
- *abstracts are often provided, lets you know if article is potentially useful*
- *connected printer saves time and effort of writing down information*
- *expanded search capabilities lets you narrow your search*
- *provides current news and information about countries and industries*
- *up to date*
- *reference numbers allow easy access to the microform business collection.*

Typical *negative comments*:

- *little product specific information*
- *limited to business and current events*
- *information goes back only to 1988*
- *relatively few entries with full text.*

NTDB. This information source was rated far and away the most useful tool. It received more comments per user and a higher proportion of positive comments than either LUIS or Infotrac (see Table 1). From the instructor's perspective, it greatly expands the international business collection of the library and makes possible informative assignments that students could not have attempted prior to the first production of NTDB in October 1990.

Typical *positive student* comments included:

- *this resource was by far the most helpful*
- *helped identify determinants of demand for our product*

- *provides product specific information on each country's major industries*
- *unsurpassed as a source for up-to-date information*
- *dramatically cut down the time required to do research*
- *reports could be copied onto diskettes, allowing students to work at their convenience, particularly important for evening students*
- *information could be edited selectively before writing final reports*
- *operation of system is painless for those with knowledge of CD-ROM operating procedures*
- *NTDB should be used first, then complemented with other sources*
- *should be required–using the system will produce better quality papers*
- *extensive statistical information*
- *files can be retrieved easily into WordPerfect*
- *should meet vast majority of user's needs*
- *gave other relevant factors such as the economic, political and financial state of each country*
- *[CD-ROM] searches are rapid*
- *keyword searchable*
- *helped to make realistic generalizations*
- *gives foreign contacts such as distributors and government agencies.*

Typical *negative comments* included:

- *you need an IBM compatible to take files away from the library*
- *most difficult to use of computerized sources–menus are not of much use to an unfamiliar researcher*
- *very little instruction information available; took work and patience to learn how to use effectively*
- *system had to be booted each time to use the program–time consuming.*

Export To Win! The evaluation indexes for *Export To Win!* are favorable (see Table 1). Of 14 student teams, only two teams had more negative comments than positive comments. Furthermore, three of the teams were "ecstatic" in their remarks; they had nothing negative to say about the simulation.

Typical *positive comments* were:

- *"The program did cover much information that wasn't presented in the text or in class. And even though we criticized the program for being too book-like, it is still a superior to a textbook as a means of instruction."*
- *"There was one final lesson that the software brought home; players that do their homework will be the ones that end up with the highest sales."*
- *"The simulation really kept our interest. We especially enjoyed the high-quality graphics; watching our ship sink taught us the value of insurance!"*
- *The software is full of information. Whoever put this simulation together spent a lot of time with details. Each student should be required to use this simulation."*
- *"As an educational tool the program achieves and surpasses its objectives. The game serves its purpose because there are explanations for terms a student will continuously find in research for the class project and in the textbook. For example, if you asked for an explanation of shipping terms, you were given graphics plus a description of the shipping terms and advantages/disadvantages. This made learning fun."*

Some typical *negative comments* were:

- *"Once a decision is made, you can't go back and reevaluate the decision. The simulation only allows you to go forward. Also, by not allowing us to back up, we found that we couldn't go back and check the meaning of previously covered terms like F.O.B. and F.A.S."*
- *"Other than the memos from the boss and the number crunching at the end of each year, the program was basically a reading assignment."*
- *"We should be allowed to make mistakes. If we select an ill-advised decision, the computer program will inform us of such and basically will not allow us to make the decision."*

- *"The manual was short and the explanations quickly got us started but it did not have much information in it about the simulation itself. It should at least include a description of the types of reports the simulation creates."*

Evaluation 2: Student Survey Rating Information Sources

LUIS. Table 2 shows the mean ratings between the four data sources on each of the previously specified criteria. LUIS had the best rating in terms of ease of use and was significantly higher than *Export To Win!*

Table 2. MEAN RATINGS OF COMPUTERIZED INFORMATION SOURCES
UTILIZED TO TEACH INTERNATIONAL BUSINESS
(Standard Deviations in Parentheses)

CRITERION	RATINGS[a]			
	LUIS	INFOTRAC	NTDB	EXPORT TO WIN
Ease of Use	32.4^b (14.5)	27.8 (10.6)	24.0 (13.6)	20.3^b (10.0)
Effectiveness	21.9^c (14.3)	23.6^c (15.6)	51.2^c (18.9)	21.6^c (12.0)
Knowledge Enhancement	17.5^d (13.2)	16.6^d (8.2)	45.3^d (19.3)	35.3^d (22.3)
Future Course Use	16.5^e (12.7)	17.7^e (11.8)	42.6^e (20.4)	33.0^e (17.46)

[a]Each student was asked to rate each computer data source on each criterion using a 100 point constant sum scale. ANOVA was performed to test for significant differences between mean ratings of data sources on each criterion. Post hoc tests, Scheffe's, were performed with alpha = .05. [b]Luis > Export to Win; [c]NTDB > all others; [d]NTDB > all others and Export to Win > Infotrac and LUIS; [e]NTDB > LUIS and Infotrac; and Export to Win > Luis and Infotrac.

The latter, however, is to be expected since LUIS is simply an on-line catalogue system whereas *Export To Win!* is a reasonably sophisticated simulation that requires some investment in "start-up" time. LUIS did not fare as well on the other three criteria and received the lowest rating in terms of future emphasis in course use.

Infotrac. Infotrac had the second highest rating in terms of ease of use (see Table 2) but was significantly lower than the NTDB in terms of effectiveness of aiding the students to complete their assigned project. Infotrac also received relatively low ratings on general knowledge enhancement and its emphasis in the course in the future.

NTDB. NTDB is clearly a "winner" according to data presented in Table 2. It was overwhelmingly rated as the superior data source in terms of effectiveness in completing the course project as well as general enhancement of international business knowledge and, was significantly greater than everything other than *Export To Win!* in terms of emphasis in the course in the future.

Export To Win! Data shown in Table 2 also confirm that *Export To Win!* is perhaps a worthy consideration for teachers of International Business. It was rated as relatively easy to use, and significantly better than LUIS and Infotrac in terms of enhancement of general knowledge of international business as well as consideration for future course use. It was not rated as highly on the effectiveness in completing the course project criterion, but several evaluators noted that it may have received a higher rating had they been introduced to the simulation earlier in the semester.

CONCLUSIONS

First, a comment relative the students' overall experience with traditional information sources and the computerized information sources they were introduced to in this project. Students' comments were overwhelmingly appreciative of the speed and ease of retrieval of the computerized information relative to traditional sources. While Infotrac, for example, provides titles, authors, dates and sources for all information, students found that those articles with abstracts provided were by far the most helpful. If material did not have an associated abstract, the student would have to find the material either in hard copy or microform. Judging from comments, the time expended in "trudging the floors" of the library is now a substantial cost for the computer literate student. However, readers should note that many evaluations, mostly negative, related to the "process" of using the four information sources. By "process" we mean the institutional procedures that are set up to determine how the information source is accessed, used, and supported. Since the "process" is unique to the authors' university, these evaluative statements were omitted from this paper. Nevertheless, potential users should be warned that a positive experience with computerized information sources can quickly turn negative if certain "process" issues are not dealt with adequately. Examples are having enough computers available, providing appointments for use of limited access sources, having printers on-line, having a supply of disks available for downloading information, and having an adequate number of qualified reference librarians available. Therefore, the authors' first suggestion is that you investigate the support your institution offers for computerized information sources and then, by all means, expose your students to the sources.

Based on the student evaluations and the authors' own experience throughout the semester, we can offer several suggestions regarding the four computerized data sources selected for evaluation in this study for use in the International Business course. In terms of the on-line library catalogue system, even though LUIS received the poorest evaluations from the students, we recommend a review of the availability and use of your university's on-line catalogue system. There are two reasons for this: (a) some of the student teams that did make use of LUIS reported that much of the information they located through LUIS was used as very good supporting information for data collected through other sources and (b) it is likely that many of your students will be unfamiliar with their own library's catalogue system; the little time spent reviewing the system is well worth the cost. LUIS is maintained by the State University System. There are no user charges associated directly with the International Business course.

Our third suggestion is that potential teachers of International Business should probably not suggest using Infotrac given an assignment similar to the one we described herein. The student evaluations of Infotrac were marginal. Here again, we offer a caveat to our own suggestion. Infotrac is one of the most popular databases at our University. Our current hardware configuration has four of the library's CD-ROM-capable personal computers running Infotrac. Given the wide student interest (extending beyond business courses) in this database, these machines are in almost constant use. Its popularity with so many students causes a common student criticism: scarcity of time available to work on the machine. If your university has Infotrac and several machines, or perhaps a central file server with several terminals networked to it, you may want to consider using Infotrac, particularly if you do not have access to NTDB. From the perspective of the business librarian, Infotrac is relatively expensive, with typical academic packages ranging from $8,000 to $24,000 per year.

The fourth suggestion is that NTDB is an ideal resource for students in the International Business class. It provides more up-to-date information than is possible with a textbook. It contains enough information to permit consideration of virtually any country, product or service. Perhaps most importantly, we have found that NTDB eliminates the old International Business term paper mentality, where students struggle to find adequate country information and then fabricate a business plan based on out-of-date, possibly not comparable, product information from other markets. NTDB permits students to engage in a realistic business planning exercise, with enough information to be able to discriminate meaningfully between countries and markets. The difference is readily apparent in their knowledgeable and detailed presentations to the "management committee." NTDB is also cheap, costing only $35 per CD-ROM, with an annual subscription rate of $360 (12 monthly updates).

Finally, we were pleasantly surprised with the student evaluations of *Export To Win!* It appears that this is a valuable learning tool for students. It complements textbook presentations well, letting students cover otherwise mundane details in an interesting simulation. We would use this program relatively early in the semester. It is available for adoption from South-Western Publishing Company.

REFERENCES

Churchill, G.A., Jr. (1991). *Marketing Research: Methodological Foundations.* Chicago: The Dryden Press.
Evans, J. and Skadden, D. (1990). *Proposed Revised Accreditation Standards, AACSB Accreditation Task Force.* St. Louis, MO: American Assembly of Collegiate Schools of Business (Monograph).
Hawkins, R.G. (1984). International Business in Academia: The State of the Field. *Journal of International Business Studies* (Winter), 15(3), 13-18.
Information Access Company. *Infotrac.* Foster City, CA.
Johnson, H.W., Faria, A.J. and Maier, E.L. (1984). *How to Use the Business Library: With Sources of Business Information,* 5th ed. Cincinnati: South-Western Publishing Co.
LUIS: Library User Information Service, Release 3.3 (1985). SUS Databases: State University System of Florida.
Nehrt, L.C. (1987). The Internationalization of the Curriculum. *Journal of International Business Studies* (Spring), 18(1), 83-90.
Strategic Management Group, Inc. (1991). *Export To Win!* Cincinnati: South-Western Publishing Co.
Thanopoulos, J. (1987). International Business Education in AACSB Schools. *Journal of International Business Studies* (Spring), 18(1), 91-98.
U.S. Department of Commerce, Economics and Statistics Administration, Office of Business Analysis. *National Trade Data Bank.* Washington D.C.

Simulating the Global Market Place:
A Software Review and Comparison

J. A. F. Nicholls
Lucette B. Comer

SUMMARY. This review discusses one simulation that has potential value as an aid in teaching international business: *The Management of Strategy in a Global Market Place*. The review describes the flow of decisions in the simulation, the interaction of the environment with the decision variables, and discusses both computer aspects and associated role play. Student evaluations of an earlier version are presented and a comparison made to another new simulation, *Export To Win!*

OVERVIEW OF THE SIMULATION

This review describes a microcomputer simulation, *The Management of Strategy in a Global Market Place*, that has great promise

J. A. F. Nicholls and Lucette B. Comer are affiliated with Florida International University College of Business Administration, Department of Marketing & Business Environment, Miami, FL 33199.

[Haworth co-indexing entry note]: "Simulating the Global Market Place: A Software Review and Comparison." Nicholls, J. A. F., and Lucette B. Comer. Co-published simultaneously in the *Journal of Teaching in International Business* (The Haworth Press, Inc.) Vol. 4, No. 3/4, 1993, pp. 135-145; and: *Utilizing New Information Technology in Teaching of International Business: A Guide for Instructors* (ed: Fahri Karakaya and Erdener Kaynak) The Haworth Press, Inc., 1993, pp. 135-145. Multiple copies of this article/chapter may be purchased from The Haworth Document Delivery Center. Call 1-800-3-HAWORTH (1-800-342-9678) between 9:00 - 5:00 (EST) and ask for DOCUMENT DELIVERY CENTER.

135

for teaching international business (IB). The simulation was originally modelled on the American economy (Cadotte 1990), but has now been expanded to encompass a global perspective. It is elaborate, with great attention to detail. In manufacturing and distributing their products worldwide, participants are drawn into a complex web of decision making. The simulation allows participants, working in teams, to plan and implement business strategies. They establish their own companies, analyze their markets, and develop corporate strategy. They design and produce their own branded products, which compete against the products of other teams in the international market place.

The simulation makes it possible for students to consider global environmental factors (e.g., economics, cultures) that establish a framework for the decision making process. Students make a set of sub-decisions involving world-wide operations: production, distribution, marketing, and finance. Students seek to optimize their company's performance within a web of decisions.

The simulation revolves around five regions of the world. These regions represent loosely aligned combinations of geographic areas, ranging in size from a portion of a continent (e.g., Western Europe) to an entire continent (e.g., South America), thus encompassing widely diverse markets. There are four cities within each region. Participants manufacture products in one or all of the regions and distribute them in as many as 20 cities worldwide. For example, products might be manufactured in Western Europe and marketed to cities in the same region (e.g., London, Oslo), or transported to cities in other regions (e.g., Mexico City, Hong Kong).

Participants face much the same problems that international managers actually confront. When establishing production sites, they must consider local industrial capabilities in the region; when choosing distribution locations, they must consider the needs and preferences of consumers from a variety of cultural backgrounds. They must also factor in the logistics of moving products between production sites and distribution centers.

The Basic Simulation

At the start of the simulation, participants undertake a market opportunity analysis. The simulation allows them to design their own research to identify customer needs and wants. In this way they are able to discover preferences, usage patterns, purchase intentions, and demographic characteristics. They can identify user segments in the different cities and estimate the relative size and potential of each. They then decide which segments and regions to target.

For simplicity, all participating teams produce and market a single generic product–microcomputers. However, the microcomputer is a multifaceted item that allows for considerable product differentiation. Based on the results of their market analysis, participants design their own brand(s) to match the requirements of their markets. They are able to assemble products with a variety of attributes, chosen from an extensive list of features. For instance, a company can produce an entry level machine (e.g., 8088 processor, monochrome monitor, 20MB hard drive) and/or more sophisticated models (e.g., 486 processor, 33MHz, XGA monitor, 320MB hard drive, modem).

They then select locations for manufacturing facilities in one, or all, of the five geographic regions and construct their plants. Expenditures vary from region to region, based on availability and costs of labor, capital, and technology. Participants may locate warehouses close to the plants in each region and distribute products from factory to warehouse to retail outlets. They must consider the trade-offs between production efficiency and distribution costs when they locate their manufacturing facilities. At the store level, they deal with many details including the size of the sales force, "point of purchase" (POP) display, and shelf space allocation. Participants develop their own advertising plans, create the actual copy, select specific print media, and decide on the number of insertions of each advertisement.

Financial considerations underlie all of these decisions. Participants arrange financing for their own operations, whether through equity issues, bank loans, or sales revenues. They consider how best to generate revenues, while simultaneously controlling the costs of production and distribution. They develop budgets for each quarter of operation with the aid of a template of spreadsheets. Although they should stay within their budgets, emergency loans are available (at usurious interest rates). In the event that they have generated excess cash flow, they have the alternative of investing in short term

CDs. Exchange rates are explicitly considered. These are controlled by the instructor, who can vary them from quarter to quarter, perhaps mirroring current political or economic conditions. This detail solidifies the participants' understanding of the financial underpinnings of a multinational corporation. To help them with their decisions, participants receive income statements, balance sheets, and cash flow analyses each quarter. Fluctuating exchange rates are reflected in the quarterly financial statements, adding another dimension of reality.

Cultural Issues

One of the most important aspects of doing business globally is understanding cultural variations from country to country. The author has made a serious effort to model such differences that may affect demand for microcomputers, working with consultants in each locale. As a result, some differences in preference segments emerge among the regions. For example, several segments for microcomputers found in China are similar to those in other countries (e.g., people who need workstations, people who want a basic machine), but one other segment is virtually unknown (persons who require portability). By careful market analyses, students can detect the presence or absence of these or other segments in the five regions.

In keeping with today's emphasis, the simulation allows participants to control the quality of their product. Preferences for quality vary globally. In Eastern Europe, for example, consumers may be perfectly satisfied with a machine with a 70% quality rating, but this would be totally unacceptable to customers in the United Kingdom. Segments that are otherwise identical in needs may differ significantly between countries because of this quality issue. Participants produce their brands at appropriate quality levels. Producing better quality machines, however, adds to costs.

Phases of the Simulation

The simulation is modeled in three years, exposing the student to distinctively different operational tasks (Table 1). The first year represents an "emergence" or "getting started" phase. During this first

Table 1

Phases of the Simulation Showing the Complex Flow of Decisions

	Emergence	Development	Maturity
Time Frame	First Year (Quarters 1 to 4)	Second Year (Quarters 5 to 8)	Third Year (Quarters 9 to 12)
Primary Concern	Getting started	Expanding operations	Extending global reach
Marketing	Design market survey Analyze market opportunities Select markets Design one or two brands Promotion: design ad copy, plan shelf allocations, POP displays Test market Enter initial markets	Begin global roll out Evaluate initial strategies Expand product line Target new segments/regions Promotion: develop media schedules, improve ad copy, shelf allocations, POP displays	Expand global roll out Evaluate brand mix Add new brands Promotion: refine media strategy, ad copy, shelf allocations, POP displays
Production	Select initial plant location(s) Construct first facilities Consider R&D alternatives	Reevaluate plant locations and capacity Construct new plants Enlarge older plants Invest in R&D	Expand factories Consider buying/selling plants Invest in R&D
Finance	Establish budgets Develop pricing strategy Obtain initial financing	Monitor and revise budgets Obtain supplementary funding	Monitor and revise budgets Consider further equity/debt financing
Competition	Monitor/counter competitors' actions	Monitor/counter competitors' actions	Monitor/counter competitors' actions Negotiate, merge and/or acquire other companies

year, participants can research the global market, design their products, locate and construct their production facilities, and test market their new brands. They are primarily concerned about getting their companies off the ground and operating profitably. The second year is a "development" phase. Participants can normalize operations and become accustomed to making decisions. They begin their global "roll out" into broader markets. As operations become profitable, they may decide to expand their product line, adding brands targeted to different segments or different parts of the world. They may become aware of the activities of their competition and find out how successful they have been in their initial strategies. By the third year, a "maturity" phase, things move much faster. Students become even more aware of the complexities and the possibilities of the simulation. They can monitor each other's operations, and lodge complaints against competitors when they suspect questionable actions.

RUNNING THE SIMULATION

Computer Aspects

Instructions for running the simulation are spelled out in detail in the *Instructor's Manual.* Participants enter their own decisions directly into the computer, using a preprogrammed diskette created by the instructor. The instructor then runs each period's decisions using the students' diskettes. "What if" analyses are available, so participants can fine tune their decisions, aided by a menu system. The *Student Manual* is very thorough and includes an extensive selection of worksheets.

Role Play Aspects

The simulation provides an opportunity for role play that can add a significant dimension to the learning experience. Students develop interpersonal as well as computer skills as they interact with members of other teams face-to-face. Intercompany negotiations can add a realistic qualitative dimension. Power strategies may emerge since companies can acquire part, or all, of each other's operations. Students learn how to deal with conflict, as well as the value of cooperation. Stronger groups may absorb the weak, so students can observe the consequences of inefficient management. Licensing arrangements are also possible. Companies can license technological components from a competitor–at a price. Participants may formalize these agreements through actual written contracts.

Competitors can monitor each others' activities and lodge complaints when they believe advertising is deceptive or misleading. Investigative hearings can be held when a complaint arises. Guilty offenders may face heavy penalties (e.g., fines, bans on advertising), at the instructor's discretion. International differences in the definition and legality of "deception" in advertising might add spice to the role play.

The degree of involvement in the role play by the instructor has a bearing on the success of the simulation. The instructor must preside over all companies as the chairman of the board and may also assume the ancillary position of adjudicator when formal complaints are lodged. S/he can conduct hearings, read evidence submitted by participants, decide guilt or innocence, and impose penalties, as appropriate.

EFFECTIVENESS OF THE SIMULATION

We obtained some indication of the potential effectiveness of the simulation by examining student's open-ended comments about an earlier version. Their responses were remarkably consistent. The nature of the comments were:

- *Provided a realistic (real world) experience [89%]*
  Participants felt that the simulation provided a realistic experience for them. They felt that they gained remarkable insight into business operations, acclimating them to pressures, and providing hands-on experience. This "real world" aspect seemed to be the predominant attraction in the students' minds.
- *Learned more than in other courses [71%]*
  Participants felt that they had learned a good deal more than in a traditional course. They also found it to be an intensely satisfying learning experience, possibly because they were "enthusiastic" and "excited" about it.

- *Integrated knowledge [36%]*
  Some participants commented that the simulation helped them integrate the knowledge that they had gained in other courses. It gave them the opportunity to apply what they had learned and to see how things worked together.
- *Learned about interpersonal relationships [29%]*
  Interestingly, some students reported that they learned a good deal about interacting with others both within their team and in their negotiations with competing teams. These students felt that learning to work together was an important aspect of preparation for their future careers. They also commented that the opportunity to negotiate and make business deals was invaluable.
- *Invested much time [82%]*
  The simulation was so all-encompassing that the students willingly committed an enormous amount of time to it. The mean average time that they reported was 18.6 hours per week. This suggests that the simulation would be most appropriately positioned as an honors course or should carry extra credit.

COMPARISON WITH "EXPORT TO WIN!"

Export To Win! (1991) is another new simulation package available as an aide to teaching IB. This simulation serves a different teaching function and is based upon a different learning philosophy. *Export To Win!* is not a simulation in which student teams compete against each other. A single student manages an export department and is guided through the simulation by memoranda and dialogue boxes, but has limited ability to make decisions. Decisions tend to be qualitative rather than quantitative. The program is really an explication of the export marketing process. *Export To Win!* is colorful and features gorgeously variegated dialogue boxes.

The two simulations are compared in Tables 2 and 3. Table 2 shows the hardware requirements for both programs. *The Global Market Place* requires more powerful computers, while *Export To Win!* only needs an entry level machine. However, to fully appreciate the latter program, a color monitor is necessary. Table 3 presents information that would be useful to instructors considering using simulation in their courses. *The Global Market Place* is targeted to a

Table 2

A Comparison between _The Global Market Place_ and _Export to Win!_

Minimum Hardware Requirements

	The Global Market Place	_Export to Win!_
Instructors' Computer Needs	80386 microprocessor Monochrome monitor Hard drive and 2 floppy drives	Not applicable
Students' Computer Needs	80286 microprocessor Monochrome monitor 1 floppy drive	8088 microprocessor Color monitor 1 floppy drive

Table 3
Comparison of *The Global Market Place* and *Export to Win!*
Course and Time Requirements

	The Global Market Place	Export to Win!
Appropriate course	Capstone IB course; Executive Training Program.	Introductory IB course.
Learning focus	Integration of knowledge necessary to run a company in a competitive global market. Deals with all corporate operations.	Development of knowledge necessary to run an export department. Deals only with export function.
Instructor's responsibilities	Considerable: Sets up and runs simulation; prints results; adjudicates disputes.	Minimal: Student works independently at own pace.
Start up time	Simulation builds from less complex to more complex decisions over the first four quarters, then continues at the same level of complexity.	Immediate start. Trial module available to learn simulation options.
Time required by simulation	At least 10-12 hours weekly. (May go higher depending on student involvement).	Open-ended; individually paced.
Teaching Materials	Student Manual (330 pp.) Instructor's Manual (152 pp.)	Student Manual (63 pp.) Instructor's Guide (18 pp.)
Maximum decision periods	12 (quarters)	5 (years)

capstone IB course whilst *Export To Win!* is aimed towards an introductory one. *The Global Market Place* requires a great deal of time commitment by faculty and students alike, while *Export To Win!* is designed for independent use by the student, and requires little or no faculty involvement.

The Global Market Place requires interaction among student teams, while *Export To Win!* is designed as a stand alone exercise for individual learning. *The Global Market Place* requires considerable prior knowledge in all business fields. The students must integrate this knowledge within a company decision framework. *Export To Win!* on the other hand, assumes no prior knowledge and walks students through some very basic concepts via programmed learning. *The Global Market Place and Export To Win!* are quite different and in no way can be considered substitutes for each other.

CONCLUSION

The Management of Strategy in a Global Market Place offers considerable potential as a teaching aid, although its implementation requires considerable commitment on the part of both instructors and students. Given such a commitment, we feel that the simulation can greatly enhance the students' learning experience, allowing them to experience the entire process of operating their own companies and of marketing their own products worldwide. Students also need to have considerable background in the business disciplines before undertaking this simulation. For this reason, we recommend the simulation for use in an advanced IB course in a University. Although our experience is more directly relevant to the University setting, we also believe that the simulation has great potential for use by industry in training fledgling managers for international operations.

REFERENCES

Cadotte, Ernest R. (1990), *The Market Place: A Strategic Marketing Simulation*, Homewood, IL: Richard D. Irwin.
Export To Win! (1991), Student Edition, developed by Strategic Management Group in cooperation with the Port Authority of NY and NJ, Cincinnati, OH: South-Western Publishing Co.

Software Applications
for International Business Education:
A Review of Compact Disclosure
and Disclosure/Worldscope Software

John William Clarry

International business education has grown considerably in the U.S. since the 1980s. Under pressures from the AACSB and American firms facing greater foreign competition, many U.S. business schools have increased their commitment and faculty teaching internationally oriented courses. However, these favorable academic trends toward internationalizing business curricula have often been constrained by the priorities of functional academic departments and the limited information or materials available on international firms. While the AACSB has generally decided to work through existing functional departments to encourage internationalization, and many book publishers have filled the gap of

---

Address all correspondence to John William Clarry, Assistant Professor of Business, Upsala College, East Orange, NJ 07019.

[Haworth co-indexing entry note]: "Software Applications for International Business Education: A Review of Compact Disclosure and Disclosure/Worldscope Software." Clarry, John William. Co-published simultaneously in the *Journal of Teaching in International Business* (The Haworth Press, Inc.) Vol. 4, No. 3/4, 1993, pp. 147-156; and: *Utilizing New Information Technology in Teaching of International Business: A Guide for Instructors* (ed: Fahri Karakaya and Erdener Kaynak) The Haworth Press, Inc., 1993, pp. 147-156. Multiple copies of this article/chapter may be purchased from The Haworth Document Delivery Center. Call 1-800-3-HAWORTH (1-800-342-9678) between 9:00 - 5:00 (EST) and ask for DOCUMENT DELIVERY CENTER.

147

teaching materials, there are still only limited data sources on international business.

The pedagogical subject of teaching international business has gradually been transformed as courses are incorporated into the functional departments of major business schools, and the emphasis of international business courses has shifted to focus more on the strategies and contingencies of multinational firms (Peterson and Mueller, 1989). In numerous texts and current courses, there is correspondingly less primary attention given to the broad international trade environment between countries. Although this shift to focus on the multinational firm has sparked pedagogical and ideological debates (e.g., Behrman and Grosse, 1991), it has also created a parallel need for more specific information about the complex international functions and processes of multinational firms.

The trends toward more international business education have overlapped an interdisciplinary increase in both information needs and database supplies. Accounting and management information systems have assumed new significance in coordinating business firms. Finance and strategic management students now commonly use online databases like Compustat from Standard & Poors or other sources (Young, 1989) to study issues in their disciplines. But unfortunately, students of international business have been relatively late to enjoy the benefits of vast databases, whether online or in published forms. Older international databases available (e.g., World Bank) often focused on the economic and political variables of nations, rather than the firms that compete or invest there. Most financial databases have a domestic bias (Choi, 1988), due to a paucity of current updated information for an international perspective. The limited information on international firms has allowed more theoretical perspectives to prevail; but now there are sufficient international business databases available for students to undertake research projects that will test or translate these academic theories into more operational and functional guidelines. This paper will discuss some of the software features of two current business databases, and then suggest some possible project applications that will complement and internationalize the functional basis of most business schools.

INTERNATIONAL BUSINESS DATABASES

There are now many different online and computerized (CD/ROM) databases available for professional and academic business uses (Young, 1989). Some of these databases are more specialized or accessible than others, depending upon the resources of an institution and the computer proficiencies of students. In this age of computer skills and capabilities, most students will have at least minimal exposure to word processing and accounting programs. Moreover, many students will often prefer information that they can search for and compile themselves from various computerized databases, even if the same information is available in text forms. In order to incorporate and apply these skills for international business course projects, this paper will discuss two computerized databases generally available for academic research or educational purposes in many institutions; they are also available online through the Nexus service.

Compact Disclosure

The CD/ROM databases of Compact Disclosure have been available in many academic and research institutions since 1986. The Disclosure universe is based on information compiled primarily from Securities and Exchange Commission (S.E.C.) filings. There are monthly discs provided by annual subscription with current information on over 10,000 publicly listed companies, updated on a regular basis. Due to SEC filing variations, there is some fluctuation of companies listed in each monthly disc; but the total number of records available provides a wealth of readily available and timely data for many student projects. Much of this information is compiled from each subject company's annual report or 10-K filings; but students often prefer the ease and user control of searching for their data through by menus, rather than using other hardcopy sources.

One of the strengths of Compact Disclosure's database products is the sophisticated and user friendly software included. Students can easily search the complete database by a number of different criteria such as company names, types of business classified by

Standard Industrial Classification (SIC) two or four digit codes, textual descriptions of businesses, or industry groups. More specific search criteria for international business include country of parent incorporation and national currency listings. Financially oriented students can also search for samples of companies with specified performance, asset, or stock market data ranges. Accounting students can examine companies by auditor or the content of auditor reports. Management students can search for companies by their number of employees or dates of recent acquisitions, or by the names and compensation levels of a firm's upper echelons of top officers.

The Disclosure software also allows student users to conduct multiple step searches, either narrowing or augmenting their searches by listing additional search criteria. For example, students may begin by searching for all companies listed in a given business code or group; then perform additional searches by setting financial ranges or by other keywords from the corporate textual fields. While there are some restrictions on search procedures, users can also follow their own customized steps through Disclosure's "emulation" mode for more flexible searches. There is also a great deal of flexibility in the display of selected data after the search is completed. Formats can be specially designed and easily edited to display only desired data, which can be presented in user display formats or downloaded into report arrangements for further analysis.

Despite the ease and sophistication of Compact Disclosure's software, there are still some inherent limitations in the database for international business students. First, since the universe is drawn from SEC filings, most of the firms in the large database are U.S. owned. There are over 300 non-U.S. owned firms that have filed American Depository Receipts (ADRs) in the U.S., but this is still only a small proportion of all companies in Disclosure's population, and could create significant biases. Moreover, there are often more missing data for non-U.S. companies because of different legal disclosure requirements. Separate databases on Canada and Europe have been created and marketed by Disclosure, but the main product is still based on U.S. SEC filings. Finally, there are few specifically international statistics included in Disclosure's financial data for either U.S. or non-U.S. companies. In order to compensate for this omission, Compact Disclosure has recently formed a joint venture with another information firm to market another more international database.

Disclosure/Worldscope

The national limitations of Compact Disclosure's database are now offset by a new product jointly developed by Disclosure and Wright's Investors Service. Wright's had previously marketed bound Worldscope volumes with international business data, and still publishes these volumes; but many students will find the new computerized access more useful and flexible. After offering a less flexible and successful product with Lotus, the Wright's firm entered a joint venture with Compact Disclosure to market Worldscope products on CD/ROM disc.

The Disclosure/Worldscope database has many of the same features and software advantages as the Compact Disclosure product discussed above. But in addition, Worldscope offers much more data on non-U.S. companies. The countries covered include not only the more developed OECD countries, but also fast growing nations like Hong Kong, Malaysia, Mexico, Singapore, and South Africa. This broader universe of nations provides a more comprehensive selection of companies to study, and can help to overcome some ethnocentric biases and information blinders of U.S. students.

While the broader universe of non-U.S. companies offers a better basis for teaching international business, the differences in accounting practices and legal disclosure requirements make direct data comparisons more difficult. The Global Disclosure/Worldscope database tries to follow a unified format to adjust data for consistency, but does not attempt to "adjust away" for any country specific accounting variations (Disclosure/Worldscope, 1991). However, there are still some national and firm-specific differences in reporting and accounting which must be kept in mind to discourage too many crude comparisons of data by students (cf. Eiteman and Stonehill, 1989: Chapters 19-20). Detailed financial footnotes of accounting adjustments are provided. Some currency adjustments for non-U.S. companies are also necessary as key financial data are usually presented in the local currency of the company for the past 10 years; but summary financial data are presented in U.S. dollar terms, and performance ratios are not impacted by different currency denominations. A valuable feature for time series analysis of non-U.S. firms is Disclosure/Worldscope's inclusion of monthly and annual foreign exchange rates to convert local currency data to U.S. dollars.

The most valuable feature of Disclosure/Worldscope for students is the easy availability of numerous foreign and international business statistics for both U.S. and non-U.S. companies. Figure 1 summarizes most of the international data available on both databases. In addition to annual international business data, there are also five year averages and growth rates reported for comparison. Although some companies do not always report all these data for public access, there are often sufficient numbers provided for a given year or total worldwide performance to determine a reasonable international business profile. Other financial information is also reported on R & D or cashflow as a percentage of sales, sales per employee, and numerous additional financial performance measures on both annual and five year average bases. Despite occasional or systematic data omissions by some companies, this kind of

FIGURE 1

INTERNATIONAL DIMENSIONS OF TWO SAMPLE DATABASES

DIMENSION	COMPACT DISCLOSURE	G L O B A L DISCLOSURE/WORLDSCOPE
Sample Size	10,000+	6000+
Update frequency	Monthly	Monthly
Universe Coverage	Public S.E.C. Listing	Wright's Investor Service
Nationalities	Mostly U.S. firms and American Deposits (ADRs)	Firms in 25 Nations 24 Industries
Time Periods	Quarterly, Annual,5 years	Annual, 5 Year Averages
Variables	Currency (Non-U.S.)	F o r e i g n S a l e s (Percentage)
	Subsidiary List	F o r e i g n A s s e t s (Percentage)
	Text Dictionary (Nation)	F o r e i g n I n c o m e (Percentage)
	Corporate Exhibits	Foreign Income Growth
	Financial Footnotes	Foreign Income Margin Foreign Return on Assets Foreign Asset Growth/Turnover Foreign Sales Growth

information is highly appreciated by international business students. It is also valuable evidence for growing numbers of non-U.S. students in MBA programs, who may be more interested in the relative performance and conduct of familiar national firms.

While the Disclosure/Worldscope product offers several features and a broader universe of global companies not accessible to Compact Disclosure users, there are still some software disadvantages for international business students. First, there are many different data fields available to users; but not all of them can provide a basis for sorting or reporting records. For particular relevance, these formatting options are not available for foreign business statistics or many financial liquidity ratios. Second, the keyword textual field searching capability is not as useful as it is with Compact Disclosure because there isn't much textual material included from annual reports, except occasional financial or accounting footnotes. Third, there are few ownership or subsidiary listings included for comparison of corporate governance or international organizational arrangements. Finally, this database is new and relatively expensive for many educational institutions to afford at a time of fiscal austerity and academic retrenchment. Unfortunately, despite a heightened interest in international business education, many universities may be unlikely to subscribe to both of these databases. Hence, students and faculty will have to learn how to either maximize the utility of what information is available, or appeal to Disclosure to broaden the availability of foreign business statistics, or to lower prices below currently reduced academic rates.

FUNCTIONAL APPLICATIONS
OF COMPUTERIZED DATABASES

The increased access to information on international business databases should help stimulate interdisciplinary interest in the theories and practices of firms involved in international business. However, the focus and applications of these computerized databases will still be shaped by the existing functional orientations that students and academic departments continue to follow, even as business schools become more internationalized. In order to justify some of the resources and support required for international business databases, specific functional projects should be designed and assigned to students which will help integrate and complement the thrust of international courses within the framework of existing business school curricula. In Figure 2, we suggest some functional projects that students can use these international business databases for.

FIGURE 2

FUNCTIONAL INTERNATIONAL BUSINESS PROJECT APPLICATIONS

Marketing   **Database Variables**

Competitor Analysis   SIC Groups, Product Segments
International Sales Profiles   Foreign Sales, Income %
                                        Foreign Subsidiary Listing
Geographic Configuration   Foreign Assets, Margin, ROA
Trends, Strategies   5 Year Foreign Averages
                                        Text Keywords and Exhibits

Management

Employment Profiles   Number of Employees
Productivity   Employee/Sales Ratios
Top Management Control   Officers and Compensation
                                        Boards of Directors
Governance   Insider, Stock Ownership
Strategic Change   Keyword Text
                                        5 Year Foreign Averages

Finance

Risk,Corporate Performance   Foreign Business Statistics
Sources of Funds   Debt, Equity Ratios
                                        Cashflows, Foreign ROA
Use of Funds   Dividends, R & D, Capital Expenditures
Stock Listings   Stock Ownership Profile
Foreign Exchange Exposure   Footnotes on Gains/Losses

Accounting and Taxation

Different Accounting Standards   Disclosure Variations
                                        Accounting Practice Footnotes
Income Tax Rates   Payable, Deferred Taxes
                                        Pretax, Net Margins
                                        Tax Havens
Transfer Pricing Practices   Profit Ratios for Industry Comparables
Intangible Asset Values   Corporate Licensing Exhibits
                                        Keywords in Text

CONCLUSIONS

The increasing interest and popularity of international business courses in many business schools has shifted the focus and emphasis of curricular issues to the firms engaged in business transactions across national borders. In order to meet this growing student interest in international business and complement the functional orientations of their other courses, there should be greater access to and utilization of computerized databases about the operations of multinational firms. This paper has compared the software features and capabilities of two relevant databases available on CD/ROM or Nexus in many universities: Compact Disclosure and Disclosure/ Worldscope. Both databases have their strengths and weaknesses in coverage or search capabilities; but when combined, they will offer a valuable pedagogical contribution to international business students and academic or practitioner researchers. Specific functional applications were suggested for possible database use, and greater utilization will help to justify and incorporate this essential but expensive investment into international business education. Thus, the pedagogical benefits of these and other databases for international business will be more interested and better trained students, who will be aware of and prepared for the possible opportunities and threats in a more integrated and information rich world economy.

BIBLIOGRAPHY

Behrman, Jack N. and Robert E. Grosse (1991) *International Business and Governments*: Issues and Institutions. Columbia: University of South Carolina Press.
Choi, Frederick D.S. (1988) "International data sources for empirical research in financial management," *Financial Management* (Summer), pp. 80-84.
Choi, Frederick D.S. et al. (1983) "Analyzing foreign financial statements: the use and misuse of international ratio analysis," *Journal of International Business Studies* (Spring/Summer), pp. 114-131.
Daniels, John D. and Lee H. Radebaugh (1989) *International Business: Environments and Operations* (5th edition). Reading, MA: Addison-Wesley.
Disclosure/Worldscope (1991) *Disclosure/Worldscope Global: Database Supplement to Compact Disclosure User's Manual*. Bethesda, MD: Disclosure Inc.
Eiteman, David K. and Arthur I. Stonehill (1989) *Multinational Business Finance* (5th edition). Reading, MA: Addison-Wesley.
Peterson, Mark F. and Rudi Mueller (1989) "University and in-house manage-

ment education of multinational business and bank employees," *Journal of Teaching in International Business*, Vol. 1, No. 1.

Porter, Michael E. (1986) "Competition in global industries: a conceptual framework," in M.E. Porter (Ed.), *Competition in Global Industries*. Boston: HBS Press.

Wright's Investor Service (1990) *Worldscope Industrial Company Profiles*. Bridgeport, CT: WIS.

Young, Murray A. (1989) Sources of competitive data for the management strategist," *Strategic Management Journal*, Vol 10: 285-291.